Confederate
Blockade Runner

Confederate Blockade Runner

The Personal Recollections of an
Officer of the Confederate Navy

John Wilkinson

LEONAUR

*Confederate Blockade Runner: the Personal Recollections
of an Officer of the Confederate Navy*
by John Wilkinson

Published by Leonaur Ltd in 2007

Originallt published in 1877 under the title:
The Narrative of a Blockade-Runner

ISBN: 978-1-84677-330-3 (hardcover)
ISBN: 978-1-84677-329-7 (softcover)

http://www.leonaur.com

Publisher's Notes

In the interests of authenticity, the spellings, grammar and place names
used have been retained from the original edition.

The opinions expressed in this book are those of the author
and are not necessarily those of the publisher.

Contents

Preface

In deference to the judgment of two or three literary friends, I have entitled this, my first attempt at authorship, *The Narrative of a Blockade-runner.* They do not agree with Shakespeare that "a rose by any other name would smell as sweet," to the reading public; nor that it is always advisable to call a thing by its proper name. It will be seen, however, by any reader who has the patience to peruse the work, that it embraces a wider scope than its title would imply. I have endeavoured to give a full account of the passage by the U. S. fleet of the forts below New Orleans; and to contribute some facts that will probably settle the controversy, in the judgment of the reader, as to the real captors of that city.

It will be seen that I have been favoured with access to Commodore Mitchell's official report of that conflict, a document never published. The information derived from it, added to facts and circumstances coming under my personal observation, furnishes the means of laying before the public an account of that action from a new point of view.

In bearing testimony to the kind and humane treatment of the prisoners of war at Fort Warren, I perform a most grateful duty. It was my good fortune to be captured and held a prisoner, before the "retaliatory" measures were adopted by the United States Government.

I have contributed some new, and, I hope, interesting

facts about the manner in which blockade running was conducted. I cannot do better than furnish the following extract from a literary friend's letter to me in reference to this effort of mine.

> I am particularly glad, believing as I do, that such a volume will help to the production of that state of mind, North and South, which every good man wishes to see grow. It is only necessary that we shall all fall into the habit of talking and writing about war matters without feeling; that we shall forget the bitterness of the conflict in our interest in its history; and if you or I can amuse Northern readers, or entertain them with our recollections, we shall certainly leave them in a pleasanter and better state of mind than we found them in.

I should be happy to believe that I had contributed, in ever so small a degree, to this consummation so devoutly to be wished for. But I would make no sacrifice of principle nor of interest to achieve this end.

While accepting the situation consequent upon the unsuccessful appeal to arms, the Southern people do not stultify themselves by professing to renounce their conviction of their right and duty in having responded to the call to defend their respective States from invasion.

But they believe that the war was conducted by the Confederate Government in a spirit of humanity. Conceiving it to be the duty of every southern man to submit any testimony in his possession relating to this subject, and especially to the treatment of prisoners of war, I have quoted some passages from *A Vindication of the Confederacy Against the Charge of Cruelty to Prisoners*. This work was recently published by the Southern Historical Society, and was compiled by the Rev. J. Wm. Jones, D.D., author of *Personal Reminiscences of Gen. R. E. Lee*. The candid and dispassionate student of history, in seeking after the truth, should read this work before forming a judgment upon this point, which has, perhaps, caused more bitter resentments among the Northern people than all the other deplorable events of our civil strife combined.

Woodside
Amelia Co., Va.
Oct. 15th, 1876

CHAPTER 1

Organising for War

When the state of Virginia seceded from the Union, on the 17th day of April, 1861, most of her citizens, belonging to the United States Navy, resigned their commissions, and offered their services to the state of their birth. Many of them had meddled so little with politics as never even to have cast a vote; but having been educated in the belief that their allegiance was due to their state, they did not hesitate to act as honour and patriotism seemed to demand. They were compelled to choose whether they would aid in subjugating their state, or in defending it against invasion; for it was already evident that coercion would be used by the General Government, and that war was inevitable. In reply to the accusation of perjury in breaking their oath of allegiance, since brought against the officers of the Army and Navy who resigned their commissions to render aid to the South, it need only be stated that, in their belief, the resignation of their commissions absolved them from any special obligation.

They then occupied the same position towards the Government as other classes of citizens. But this charge was never brought against them till the war was ended. The resignation of their commissions was accepted when their purpose was well known. As to the charge of ingratitude, they reply, their respective States had contributed their full share towards the expenses of the General Government, acting as their disbursing agent; and when these states withdrew from the Union, their citizens belonging to the two branches of the public service did not, and do not, consider themselves amenable to this charge for abandoning their official positions to cast their lot with their kindred and friends. But yielding as they did to necessity, it was nevertheless a painful act to separate themselves from companions with whom they had been long and intimately associated, and from the flag under which they had been proud to serve.

During the brief interval which elapsed between the act of secession and the admission of the state into the Confederacy, the Virginia Army and Navy were organized; and all of the naval officers who had tendered their services received commissions in the Virginia, and afterward in the Confederate Navy; but as there were very few vessels in commission, the greater portion of these officers were ordered to shore batteries.

My first experience was at Fort Powhatan, an earthwork situated on James River a short distance below City Point, and carrying six or eight guns mounted on ships' carriages, which had been transported from the Norfolk navy yard. "Grim visaged war" had not shown his "wrinkled front" in those fair portions of the land; and our time was chiefly spent in drilling the volunteers at the big guns, and visiting the hospitable families in the neighbourhood; but all of us were soon to be transferred to more active scenes.

The young gentlemen-privates of the gallant volunteer company, who so daintily handled the side and train-tackles of the 42-pounders in the battery, considered themselves fortunate, not long afterwards, if they obtained full rations of lean beef, or "Nassau" pork, and "hard tack;" and bore the brunt of many a severely contested battle as part of Stonewall Jackson's "foot cavalry." But at this period there were only a few so called croakers who at all realized the magnitude of the struggle about to ensue. The camps resounded with song and merriment; and many of the young warriors were attended, like the knights-errant of old, by a faithful squire, who polished the boots, cleaned the musket, and performed other menial service for his "young master."

My own *fidus Achates*, was old "Uncle Billy," whose occupation was gone by the stoppage of a tobacco factory in Richmond, where he had been used to take a prominent part in the peculiar songs of the "profession." He would sometimes give us a specimen of his vocal powers, and would nearly bring the house down, literally and metaphorically, while executing the mysteries of a "Virginny breakdown" in thick soled brogans sixteen inches long.

But to return from this digression, it was believed by many persons that a large party at the North would oppose the prosecution of a war of invasion. It will be remembered by those at all conversant with the history of events at that time, how strong had been the party opposed to secession in the Convention then in session at Richmond, (at least two-thirds of its members having been elected as Union men,) and what strenuous efforts towards peace and compromise had been made by the Border States Commissioners.

The call upon Virginia, by President Lincoln, for her quota of troops to aid in subjugating the South, had settled the question, however, in the Convention; and in a few hours after Governor Letcher's reply to that call, Virginia had virtually cast her lot with the Gulf States, although two weeks elapsed before she became a member of the Confederacy.

I had visited, some months previous to the secession of the state, many of the little villages in New England, where I saw that the population were in terrible earnest. "Wide awake," and other secret societies were organized; and inflammatory harangues aroused the populace. The favourite theme of the orators was the "martyrdom" of John Brown; the piratical and murderous raid of that fanatic into the state of Virginia being exalted into a praiseworthy act of heroism.

When I returned to Virginia and contrasted the apparent apathy and want of preparation there with the state of affairs at the North, I trembled for the result. But when the state severed her relations with the Union, the Governor acted with great vigour and ability, and the most was made of the limited resources at his command. Volunteers responded with alacrity to the call to defend the state from invasion; and none responded more readily, or served more bravely, than those who had opposed secession in the Convention.

It seems invidious to cite particular examples; but the "noblest Trojan of them all" will point a moral, and serve as an exemplar for generations to come. Wise in council, eloquent in debate, bravest and coolest among the brave in battle, and faithful to his convictions in adversity, he still lives to denounce falsehood and wrong. Truly the old hero, in all he says and does, "gives the world assurance of a man."—I allude to Gen. J. A. Early.

When Fort Powhatan was abandoned, I was ordered to the command of a battery at Acquia Creek on the Potomac. Although situated upon the frontier, few incidents occurred there to vary the monotony of our lives. Occasionally some of the gunboats guarding the river would steam in, and exchange a few shots with us; and we witnessed frequent skirmishes between them and Walker's afterwards famous battery of flying artillery; but ammunition being extremely scarce at that period in the Confederacy, the orders to us were peremptory to be very sparing in the use of it.[1]

The battery at Acquia Creek was constructed at the terminus of the railroad from Fredericksburg, and was manned by an infantry company acting as artillerists. Besides this force, permanently stationed at the battery, and quartered near it, a company of infantry from military headquarters was sent every evening to guard against a night attack.

A company called the "Tigers," took their turn at this service, and we would gladly have dispensed with their "protection." Utterly undisciplined, they were more dangerous to friends than to foes. Mutinous and insubordinate, they were engaged in constant collisions with each other and with the companies so unfortunate as to be quartered near them; and their camp was a pandemonium. In addition to other sources of quarrel and contention, several women (*vivandiéres*, they called themselves) followed the company. The patience of Gen. M.[2] who commanded the division, was finally exhausted. He summoned the Captain of the "Tigers" into his presence; and after severely reprimanding him for the misconduct of his men, insisted that the *vivandiéres* should be sent away.

The captain urged many reasons for keeping them; the chief one being the good *moral effect* of their presence! But the General was inflexible. Even gallantry to the sex must be sacrificed to the truth; and a proper regard for the latter demands the statement that a reformation commenced with the departure of the women; and our friends the "Tigers" eventually became well-behaved soldiers.

We passed many months of inglorious inactivity here until the spring of 1862, when the line of the Potomac was abandoned. While the Federal forces had remained comparatively quiet in this part of the Confederacy, they had achieved many important successes elsewhere. Fort Donelson, on the Cumberland River, and Roanoke Island in North Carolina had been captured, with large garrisons; and New Orleans and Savannah were threatened. General Joseph E. Johnston, who at the time commanded the Army of Northern Virginia, determined to fall back to the line of the Rappahannock; and all the batteries on the Potomac were abandoned between the 8th and 10th of March, 1862; the guns being removed to other quarters.

The monotonous service at the batteries had tried the patience of all who were attached to them; and we rejoiced at the prospect of more active duty. The reverses sustained by the Confederate arms were not to be disguised, nor were our convictions of great danger to the country to be removed by the politic proclamation issued by the Confederate Government, to the effect that a contraction of the lines could exercise no material influence upon the issue of the war. But as it was deemed necessary by the military authorities to abandon the situation, we were not at all sorry to depart; for although we had seen no active service, insatiate war had claimed many victims, who had perished ingloriously by the malarial fevers of that marshy district.

The naval officers were especially elated at the change. Their duties and their authority being alike undefined, there resulted a deplorable want of harmony between them and the military. This was, indeed, the inevitable conse-quence of the anomalous position held by the former; and this want of concert of action subsequently contributed, in some measure at least, to the disastrous issue of the conflict below New Orleans.

We, having been trained in the strict discipline of a man of war, wanted *savoir faire* in dealing with the fastidious young captains, and the equally sensitive "high privates"; while they no doubt looked upon us as a domineering, tyrannical set of exclusives and wished that we were on board the Fed-eral gunboats in the river, or farther. My personal intercourse, however, was always very pleasant with them.

Capt. Brown, commanding the company of North Caro-linians at the battery, had graduated at the U. S. Naval School a year or two previous to the war, and was a strict disciplinarian. Two years after our separation, I fell in with him accidentally; and he then gave me a sad account of the changes wrought by death and disease in his fine company. He had risen to the rank of Colonel, and was then on his return to duty in the army of Northern Virginia after recovery from wounds received in battle. The graphic account given by him of the manner in which he was wounded and his narrow escape from death, may interest others as much as it did me.

His regiment formed part of Gen. Ed. Johnson's division, which held the salient angle in Gen. Lee's line at Spottsylvania C. H. when it was forced by the Federal troops. The attack was made at early dawn and in the additional obscurity of a Scotch mist; and so complete was the surprise according to B.'s account, that he was only made aware of the close proximity of the enemy by dimly discerning, a few paces distant, a Federal soldier with his musket levelled at him. The soldier fired, and B. fell insensible, shot through one of the lungs. Upon recovering consciousness, he found himself on a litter borne by Federal soldiers.

An officer leaned over him, and offered him some liquor from his canteen, which revived him so far that he was able to speak. His humane captor then volunteered to transmit any message to B.'s friends and relatives. While B. was rallying his failing senses to deliver what he believed to be his dying messages to the loved ones at home, a rattling fire of musketry opened upon them, the litter bearers and the officer were shot down; the latter falling across Brown, who relapsed into insensibility. When he again recovered consciousness, he found himself borne in the same litter, now carried by Confederate soldiers. The position had been retaken. His good friend had been shot dead.

Our mess at Acquia Creek was abundantly supplied with food from land and water. Every member of it, no doubt, frequently longed afterwards for the "flesh pots of Egypt." We discovered, by chance, a large bulk of coal, which had been stored on the long wharf where the Acquia Creek steamboats used to make their landings. When the Point was shelled about the commencement of the war by the gunboats, the wharf was destroyed, the coal falling uninjured ten or twelve feet to the bottom of the river. We fished up our supplies with oyster tongs as they were needed, and our snug quarters were kept warm during the winter.

Towards the end of the season, one of the mess servants lately arrived from the rural districts, was sent in the boat for a supply from the *coal mine*. He had made many a fire of soft coal in the drawing room at home; but although an accomplished servant, his education had been so far neglected that he was ignorant of all the "'ologies." He was very much astonished at our process of coal mining, and asked me with great gravity, on his return with the load, "if coal grew like that all over the Potomac." Of course I replied in the affirmative. It was anthracite hard coal, a specimen of which he had never seen; so he was further informed that it was hard or soft according to the season when it was fished up, being soft in the summer and hard in the winter. He was much pleased to have acquired all this information, and probably took the earliest opportunity, on his return home, to enlighten his circle of friends and acquaintances upon the subject of coal mining on the Potomac.

NOTES

1. The belief still prevails, probably, at the North, that extensive preparations had been made by the South for the war. But General Joseph E. Johnston who was assigned to the service of organizing and instructing the Virginia volunteers called out by Governor Letcher states the contrary. He asserts that all the arms to be depended upon at that time, were those found in the Southern arsenals, U. S. muskets, and rifles of discarded patterns to the number of about 75,000; 40,000 flint muskets belonging to the state of Virginia, and 20,000 procured for the state of Georgia by Governor Brown. It was charged that Mr. Floyd of Virginia while Secretary of War under President Buchanan had caused the removal of public arms to the Southern arsenals; but a Committee of the House of Representatives, in 1861, exonerated Mr. Floyd from the charge, and the chairman of that Committee was the Hon. Mr. Stanton, a prominent and zealous member of the Republican party. General Johnston, who was in a position to know the facts, states in his "Narrative, etc.," that the "Confederate States began the war with one hundred and twenty thousand arms of obsolete models, and seven hundred of the recently adopted weapons rifled-muskets, and the United States with about four hundred and fifty thousand of the old, and all of the modern arms that had been made since the adoption of the new models." When in August, 1861, it was in contemplation to send the Army of Northern Virginia into Maryland, want of ammunition, according to the distinguished authority just quoted, was one of the chief obstacles to the project.

2. The allusion is made to Genl. Mears, who commanded at Acquia Creek and to the Baltimore "Tigers", at the time commanded by Captain Thomas.

CHAPTER 2

Duty Afloat

I was ordered to report to Commodore Whittle, commanding the naval station at New Orleans, for duty afloat. A powerful fleet of ships of war and bomb vessels, under the command of Commodore (afterwards Admiral) Farragut, was then assembling at the mouth of the Mississippi, for an attack upon New Orleans, in which a large land force under Gen. Butler (afterwards called the Beast) was to cooperate. The citizens were under the impression that the place was impregnable. Gen. Duncan, commanding Forts Jackson and St. Philip, below the city, was considered one of the best artillerists in the service; and the land defence was entrusted to Gen. Lovell, with a well appointed force under his command.

The people of that gay city were occupied as usual in business and pleasure, and continued unconscious of their peril up to the very time when the Federal fleet passed the forts. But the condition of affairs, so far as naval defence was concerned, was lamentable. The regular C. S. naval fleet consisted of the *Louisiana* (Captain McIntosh) and carrying the flag of Commodore Mitchell; the steamer *McRae* (Captain Huger), carrying six light 32-pounders and nine-inch pivot gun; the steamer *Jackson* (Captain Renshaw), with two pivoted smooth bore 32-pounders; the small iron plated "Ram" *Manassas* (Captain Warley), carrying one 32-pounder carronade in the bow; and two launches, each carrying a howitzer and a crew of twenty men. There were also present, at the time the passage was forced by the U. S. fleet, two *Louisiana* state gunboats, viz., the *Governor Moore*, Captain Kennon, carrying two 32-pounder rifled guns, and the *General Quitman*, with a similar battery. *These* were converted sea steamers, with pine and cotton barricades to protect the more vulnerable part of their machinery.

All of the above vessels, with the exception of the *Louisiana* and *Manassas*, were too slightly built for war purposes. The unarmed steamboats, *Mozier*, placed under Commodore Mitchell's command. In addition to the above force, there were six steamers carrying from one to two guns each, constituting what was called the "River Defence Squadron," under the command of Captain Stevenson. These vessels' boilers and machinery were protected by heavy timber barricades, filled in with compressed cotton; and they were prepared with bar-iron casing around their bows to act as "Rams."

The *Louisiana* was pierced for twelve guns rifled six-inch; and eight-inch shell guns, three in the bow, three in each broadside, and three in the stern. Her armour consisted of railroad-iron bars securely bolted upon the sides and ends of the long covered box built upon her nearly submerged hull. These sides and ends sloped at an angle of about forty-five degrees; around the upper deck was a stout bulwark about five feet high, and iron plated inside, to resist grape shot, and afford a protection to the sharp-shooters stationed there in action.

The propelling power consisted of huge wheels, boxed up in the centre of the vessel; and a propeller on each quarter. A more powerful and efficient iron-clad called the *Mississippi* had just been launched from the stocks, but the passage of the forts was effected before her battery could be put on board.

After a few days' service on board the *Jackson*, I was ordered on board the *Louisiana* (as executive officer) then lying alongside the levee at New Orleans. Her battery was not mounted; and the mechanics were at work upon her unfinished armour and machinery. Much was to be done, and with the most limited facilities; but many obstacles had been surmounted and affairs were progressing favourably, when we received orders from Commodore Whittle to proceed down the river as far as the forts. Our wheels were in working order; but a great deal was to be done to the propellers, and the crew were still engaged in mounting the guns. But Commodore Whittle, though cognizant of our condition, was compelled against his judgment, to yield to the urgent telegrams of General Duncan to send the *Louisiana* down the river.

We had been unable to man the ship with sailors; for although many of this class belonged to the various volunteer companies around New Orleans, their commanding officers were not disposed to part with them; nor were the "jack tars" themselves willing to exchange camp life for the discipline and subordination of the naval service. Our regular crew being too small to man the battery, we gladly accepted the services of the "Crescent Artillery," a fine volunteer company raised in New Orleans. Two river steamboats were assigned to the *Louisiana* for the purpose of towage, if necessary, and for the accommodation of the mechanics who were still at work on board.

We cast off from the levee on Sunday, April the 20th. It was a bright day, and a large concourse was assembled to witness our departure. Steam had been got up, and as our big wheels were set in motion in the rapid current of the Mississippi, torrents of water rushed through the crevices in the bulkheads and deluged the gun deck, while the *Louisiana* drifted helplessly down the river, feeling the effect of the wheels no more sensibly than if they were a pair of sculling oars. *"Facilis descensus Averno; sed revocare gradum, hoc opus, hic labor est."* The aptness of the quotation will be appreciated by the reader who is in at the death of the *Louisiana*. We accomplished our object of getting down to the forts about seventy miles below the city, thanks to the current and our two transports; but our artillerists were in a shabby plight while trying to work the guns knee-deep in water.

Securing the *Louisiana* by hawsers to the left bank of the river near Fort St. Philip, on the morning of the 21st, we continued our labours upon the machinery and on the battery. The bombardment of the forts had been in progress for several days and nights, and the shells from the fleet were thrown with beautiful and destructive precision (some of them occasionally falling in close proximity to the *Louisiana*), while the bomb vessels themselves were beyond the range of the fort's guns. The naval officers were quite sure that an attempt would soon be made by Admiral Farragut to force the passage, and that so far as the naval strength was concerned, it was apparent our means were inadequate to prevent it.

Commodore Mitchell, on our arrival below, had delivered to Captain Stevenson written orders from General Lovell requiring him to place all the "River Defence Squadron" under the Commodore's orders. Captain S., on receiving these instructions, addressed a written communication to Commodore Mitchell, to the effect that all of the officers and crew under his command had entered the service with the distinct understanding that they were not to be placed under the command of naval officers; and that, while willing to co-operate with our forces, he would receive no orders from the Commodore nor allow any vessel under his command to do so; reserving to himself the right of obeying or disobeying any orders the Commodore might issue.

With this assumption of absolute independence, Commodore Mitchell's position was extremely embarrassing, but he did all that was then in his power. Not knowing at what moment an attack would be made, he endeavoured to agree with Captain Stevenson upon a plan of cooperation; and he states in his official report made after the action that Captain Stevenson "seemed disposed zealously to second these objects in many respects."

A few days previous to the action, I had been sent down the river to communicate, under a flag of truce, with one of the ships of the squadron; and in the course of conversation with my old friend Captain DeCamp, the officer in command of a division of the fleet had been informed by him that they could force the obstructions across the river whenever they pleased, and intended doing so when they were ready. The interview took place in his cabin; and although I indignantly repudiated the idea, I could not help feeling how confidently I would stake life and reputation upon the issue if our situations were reversed. I had noticed many familiar faces among the officers and crew as I passed along the deck a few moments before. Every one was at his station; the guns cast loose for action; and it was in the nature of things, that I should contrast this gallant man of war and all this efficiency and discipline with the iron bound box and crew of "horse marines" which I had just left. But it was in no spirit of depreciation of the gallantry of my comrades, for I was quite sure that they would stand to their guns. The wretched "bowl of Gotham" which had no efficient motive power, and which could not even be got under way, when anchored, without slipping the chain cable, caused the misgivings. It is no disparagement to the prowess of the U. S. fleet which passed the forts, to assert, that they never could have successfully opposed our forces; but the battle was won quite as effectually when they succeeded in passing beyond the range of the guns of the forts and the *Louisiana.*

After our official business was closed, DeC. and I began to talk of the war; and he expressed the opinions then entertained, beyond a doubt, by a majority of U. S. army and naval officers. They believed it to be the intention of the Government to bring the seceding States back into the Union, with their rights and institutions unimpaired. Since then a little leaven has leavened the whole lump, and the former doctrine of the extreme abolitionists has long become the creed of the dominant party. But some facts should be borne in mind by those who denounce slavery as the sum of all villainies; for instance, that the slave code of Massachusetts was the earliest in America; the cruellest in its provisions and has never been formally repealed; that the Plymouth settlers, according to history, maintained "that the white man might own and sell the negro and his offspring forever;" that Mr. Quincy, a representative from Massachusetts during the war of 1812, threatened the House of Congress that the North would secede "peaceably if we can, forcibly if we must" unless their demands for peace were acceded to; and lastly that the abolitionists of a later age denounced the Constitution and canonized John Brown for committing a number of murders and endeavouring to incite servile insurrection in time of peace. Truly *tempora mutantur*, etc.

The river obstructions, above alluded to, consisted of a line of sunken vessels, and of heavy pieces of timber chained together, and extending from bank to bank. A few days before the attack was made, General Duncan was speaking rather confidently of his barricade, when Warley remarked, "General, if I commanded a fleet below, and my commission lay above your obstructions, I would *come up and get it.*" Most of us belonging to that little naval fleet, knew that Admiral Farragut would dare to attempt what any man would; and for my own part, I had not forgotten that while I was under his command during the Mexican War, he had proposed to Commodore Perry, then commanding the Gulf Squadron, and urged upon him, the enterprise of capturing the strong fort of San Juan de Ulloa at Vera Cruz *by boarding*. Ladders were to be constructed and triced up along the attacking ships' masts; and the ships to be towed along side the walls by the steamers of the squadron. Here was a much grander prize to be fought for; and every day of delay was strengthening his adversaries. It was the general belief, indeed, at the time, that the admiral was in daily communication with the city by means of spies; and the public indignation was so deeply roused against Mr. T——t, the constructor of the *Mississippi*, ("a Northern man with Southern principles") who failed from time to time in launching that vessel as he had appointed to do, that he was in danger of *Lynch law*; and it is at least a singular coincidence that the naval attack was made immediately after that powerful vessel was launched, and before the guns could be put on board. But the idea of any collusion between Mr. T——t and the enemy, or of treachery on the part of the former, was never entertained, I believe, except by a few bigoted zealots, blinded by hate and passion against every one born north of the Potomac.

This class, which ought to have acted more fairly, found many followers among the multitude; from which little charity or justice can ever be expected. Nearly 1900 years ago the "plebes," influenced by their leaders, demanded the release of a robber and murderer and crucified the Saviour of mankind; and history further informs us that 500 years before that era, a Greek citizen could be banished without special trial, accusation, or defence; and that Aristides was sent into exile because people were tired of hearing him always called "the Just." Social ostracism will continue to exist till the millennium. The gentlemen of northern birth who were so unfortunate as to occupy prominent positions during the war, were mercilessly held up to scorn and distrust, if they failed to come up to the public expectation. In truth, they occupied trying positions; being regarded by many as aliens and mercenaries. *Mens conscia recti* will support us under many trials; but it does not furnish armour of proof against the "poor man's scorn, the proud man's contumely."

The interval between the 21st and 24th of April was occupied by Commodore Mitchell in organizing the force under his command, and in endeavouring to arrange some concert of action with the "River Defence" gunboats.

On board the *Louisiana* every effort was made to complete the works upon the propellers, and in mounting the battery, on which the mechanics worked night and day. Our "Crescent artillery;" a detachment of artillery from the forts under Lieutenant Dixon; and Captain Ryan's company of Sharp-shooters supplied the deficiencies in our crew. The Commodore was unsuccessful in his efforts to induce Captain Stevenson to employ one of his gunboats below the obstructions at night, to watch the U. S. fleet; and we had no vessel suitable for that purpose; the only one which would have answered (the Jackson) having been sent, with one of the launches, to watch the U. S. land forces near the Quarantine station, five miles above us. The only launch which remained to us was sent, by the Commodore's orders, below the obstructions every night, but the officer in command afterwards proved either a traitor or a coward, failing to make the concerted signal upon the approach of the fleet, and never reporting himself on board the *Louisiana* afterwards.

General Duncan urged upon the Commodore, the first or second day after our arrival below, to take a new position with the *Louisiana* at the river bank just below Fort St. Philip, and under cover of its guns, from whence she might open fire with effect upon the mortar fleet. The Commodore declined the proposition, and his action was sustained in a consultation with all the commanding officers of the C. S. naval forces present, on the grounds, "first, that the battery of the *Louisiana* was not in a condition for service;" "second, that the completion of the propeller and other mechanical work in progress, was indispensable to the efficiency of the vessel, and that it would be interrupted if she were placed under fire;" and third, "that placing the *Louisiana* in a position to receive the fire of the enemy, before her own battery could be served with effect, would be improperly hazarding, not only her own safety, but the security of the passage between the forts on which rested the possession of New Orleans."[3]

But on the afternoon of the 23rd the work had so far progressed as to encourage the belief that the vessel might be moved to the point proposed, and the Commodore, after making a reconnaissance, had decided to do so, and notified General Duncan of this intention. Captain Stevenson was to assist with two of his gunboats which were especially well adapted to this purpose.

Commodore Mitchell, in his official report to the C. S. Secretary of the Navy, intimates that "he fully appreciated and admitted the importance of the proposed change of position for the *Louisiana*," but contends that "the state of the battery, independent of other weighty reasons, was sufficient to prevent its being made previous to the engagement of the 24th." One of these consists in the fact, that owing to the peculiar construction of the *Louisiana*'s port-holes, her guns could not be elevated more than five degrees. The mortar fleet would have been beyond their range.

NOTES

3. From Commodore Mitchell's official report to the Secretary of the C. S. Navy, dated August 19th, 1862.

CHAPTER 3

The Destruction of the *Louisiana*

On the night of April 23d, the bursting of the shells was as incessant as usual. Toward daylight of the 24th, an ominous calm of brief duration was broken by the first broadside of the advancing fleet, which had approached so rapidly as to remove and pass the obstructions undiscovered, and before the launch on picket duty could get back to our fleet. For a few minutes the roar of the guns was deafening; but objects were so obscured by the darkness and the dense smoke, that we could only fire, with effect, at the flashes of the ship's guns. The *Louisiana's* three bow guns (one rifled seven-inch and two seven-inch shell guns) and her three starboard broadside guns (a rifled six-inch and two eight-inch shell guns) were all that could be brought to bear during the engagement; for being moored to the river bank, the stern and port broadside guns were useless.

The U. S. fleet came up in two divisions, delivering their broadsides in rapid succession. One of the ships was set on fire by one of the fireboats (a number of which had been prepared) but the flames were speedily extinguished. It is said that the unarmed tug *Mozier*, under her heroic commander, Sherman, while towing a fireboat alongside a heavy ship, was sunk by a broadside delivered at short range, all on board perishing. One of the largest ships, believed to be the *Hartford*, came in contact with our stern, and received the fire of our three bow guns while in this position, returning a broadside, but she soon swung clear of us and continued on her way up the river.

When day fairly broke, the storm had passed away, leaving wreck and ruin in its wake. The river banks were dotted, here and there, with burning steamers, and a large portion of the U. S. fleet had succeeded in getting beyond the forts. A few vessels of the attacking force had failed to pass the obstructions before daylight, and were driven back by the guns from the forts. The *Louisiana* and the *McRae* were the only vessels left to the Confederates; but the former was almost intact, her armour proving a sufficient defence against the broadsides, even when delivered at close range. The eight-inch shells of the *Hartford* buried themselves about half their diameter in our armour, and crumbled into fragments. All of our casualties occurred on the spar deck; our gallant commander being mortally wounded there; and many of the mechanics, who were quartered on board the tenders alongside of us, were killed or wounded. The *McRae* and the *Manassas* were in the stream in time to take an active part in the conflict; the former being considerably cut up. The *Manassas* struck two vessels with her prow, but did not succeed in sinking either. Having followed the fleet some distance up the river, and being hard pressed and seriously damaged, she was run ashore and abandoned. She shortly afterwards floated off and drifting down the river, sank between the forts. The *Louisiana* state gunboat *Governor Moore* made a gallant fight, sinking the U. S. gunboat *Verona*.

Kennon, in his official report, states his loss at fifty-seven killed and thirteen wounded out of a crew of ninety-three. He ran his vessel ashore when she was in a sinking condition, and set fire to her with his own hand. The "River Defence" gunboats, with the exception of the *Resolute*, were either destroyed by fire of the enemy's fleet, or by their own crews. The *Resolute* was discovered ashore, after the action, about a mile above Fort Jackson and abandoned by her crew. Lieut. Alden, with a party from the *McRae*, took possession of her, and endeavoured to get her afloat as she was very little injured, but being attacked by one of the gunboats from above, which succeeded in putting several shots through her hull at the water line, Alden was compelled to abandon her after setting her on fire. Among the mortally wounded on board the *McRae* was her commander T. B. Huger. The *Defiance*, one of the "River Defence" gunboats, escaped without material injury. She was turned over to the command of Commodore Mitchell by Captain Stevenson on the 26th, without any of her officers and crew, who refused to remain in her, and went ashore.[4]

After landing the wounded, we continued the work upon the machinery of the *Louisiana*, buoyed up by the hope of soon being able to retrieve our disasters. Our number was increased by officers and men who had escaped from some of the abandoned vessels. Many of them, to obtain shelter from the shells and canister shot of the Federal fleet, had taken refuge in the bayous which lie not far from the river in many places; and they looked like half drowned rats as they came on board the *Louisiana*. One of the officers gave a ludicrous account of a poor girl, who had fled from her home on the river bank as the fleet was passing, with no clothing except her night dress, and no earthly possession but a lap-dog which she held in her clasped arms. She had sought the same place of refuge and as the shells and shot would whistle over her head she would dive like a duck under the water; and every time she rose above the surface, the lap-dog would sneeze and whimper a protest against the frequent submersions. The officer at last persuaded her to let him take charge of her draggled pet; and finally had the pleasure of seeing her safe back to her home before leaving her.

During the night of the 27th after unremitting labour, our machinery was at last completed, and we prepared to make the attempt to go up the river in pursuit of the fleet. Commodore Mitchell notified General Duncan of his purpose, and the latter seemed sanguine of a successful issue, assuring the Commodore of his ability to hold the forts for weeks. Orders were issued on board the *Louisiana* for the crew to have an early breakfast, and every thing to be in readiness to cast off from the river bank a little after sunrise. The situation justified the hopes entertained by us of at least partially retrieving our fortunes, when, shortly after daylight, an officer came across the river to us from Fort Jackson, with General Duncan's compliments, and to say that General D. was about to surrender the forts to Commodore Porter.[5] In nautical parlance, we were "struck flat aback" by this astounding intelligence.

With the forts as a base of operations, we might repeat the effort, if the first were unsuccessful; and would be able to repair damages, if necessary, under shelter of their guns; but with their surrender we were helpless. The capture of the *Louisiana* would then become, indeed, a mere question of time, without the firing of a gun; for we would have been unable to replenish our supplies either of provisions or coal when exhausted. The most sanguine spirits on board, in the light of their experience of the motive power of the *Louisiana*, did not believe that we could accomplish more than the control of that portion of the river within the range of our guns; nor that the vessel could ever do much more than stem the rapid current of the Mississippi. The surrender of New Orleans was, indeed, inevitable; but even that catastrophe would not involve complete possession of the river by the enemy while we held the forts near its mouth. The gigantic efforts afterwards made by the Federal forces for the capture of Vicksburg showed the vital importance attached by the United States Government to the possession of the fortified positions on the Mississippi, while the equally desperate exertions made by the Confederacy to hold it, demonstrated our consciousness of its value to us.

Commodore Mitchell ordered his boat and proceeded with all haste to remonstrate with General Duncan; but all was unavailing; the General informing the Commodore that he had already dispatched a boat to the United States fleet, offering to surrender his command under certain conditions; disclaiming, in the offer, all control over the forces afloat. The

Commodore's boat had scarcely got back to the *Louisiana*, when the quartermaster on duty reported one of the ships of the fleet below steaming up the river towards us, with a white flag flying at the mast-head. General Duncan, it is said, stated to the citizens of New Orleans a few days afterward, that a large number of his guns had been spiked by the mutineers of the garrison; and that he had no alternative but to surrender.

A hasty council of war was held on board the *Louisiana*, during which it was decided to transfer the officers and crew to our two tenders and to burn the ship. This was speedily carried into effect, and the two transports steamed across the river as the flames burst through the *Louisiana*'s hatchway.[6] Those who wished to make the attempt to escape through the bayous, received permission to do so; and a few of the number, familiar with the locality, succeeded in evading the Federal pickets, and getting within the Confederate lines. The rest of us were entrapped; passing several hours of very unpleasant suspense, while the forts were being surrendered.

It was a grand spectacle when the flames reached the *Louisiana*'s magazine. The hawsers, securing her to the river-bank, having been burnt in two, she floated out into the stream a few minutes before the explosion; and at the moment of its occurrence, a column of pure white smoke shot rapidly high into the air from the blazing hull, wreathing itself at the top into the shape of a snow-white "cumulus" cloud; and in a few seconds afterwards, huge fragments of the wreck showered down, far and wide, upon the river and the adjacent shore. The *Louisiana* had disappeared before the deafening report attending the catastrophe reached our ears.

Immediately after the United States flag was hoisted upon the forts, the steamer *Harriet Lane* steamed slowly toward us, and sent a shot over our heads as a summons to haul down the Confederate flag which was then flying at our peak. The demand was promptly complied with, and we were prisoners of war.

Upon the pretext that we had violated the usages of war by burning the *Louisiana* while a flag of truce was flying, we were for a time subjected to unusual humiliations; learning afterwards, indeed, that Commodore Porter had recommended to the Secretary of the Navy a continuance of harsh treatment toward us upon our arrival at Fort Warren, where we were destined. The reply to the charge brought against us is obvious, viz., we were no parties to the flag of truce; nor were we included in the terms of the surrender; General Duncan treating only for the garrisons under his command, and expressly disclaiming any connection with us.

We were kept for a few days in close confinement on board the United States gunboat *Clifton*,[7] and were transferred from her on the 7th of May to the frigate *Colorado*, lying off the mouth of the Mississippi. Here we found Kennon, who had been consigned to a "lower deep" than ourselves. He was placed under a sentry's charge behind a canvas screen on the opposite side of the gun deck from us; and strict orders were given that no one should hold any communication with him. The charge against him was, that he had caused the death of some of his wounded crew by setting fire to his ship before their removal, a charge denied by him; but even if it were true, or admitted, that some of his crew were unable to escape, he was only responsible to his own government.

In a few days, however, he was released from solitary confinement, and many restrictions were removed from all of us. But humiliations or physical discomforts weighed as a feather upon our spirits compared with our reflections upon the consequences of the disaster which we had witnessed; and our consciousness that this sad fate had been brought upon the country chiefly by treachery and want of concert. And, indeed, the extent of the disaster could scarcely be exaggerated. It gave the United States Government possession of the state of Louisiana, the almost complete control of the Mississippi river, and separated Texas and Arkansas from the rest of the Confederacy for the remainder of the war.

NOTES

4. Extract from Commodore Mitchell's official report dated August 19th, 1862.

The following is believed to be a correct list of the vessels that passed up by Forts Jackson and St. Philip during the engagement of the 24th April; mounting in the aggregate one hundred and eighty-four guns, *viz. Hartford* steamer, 28 guns 1st class sloop. *Richmond*, 28; *Brooklyn*, 28; *Pensacola*, 28; *Mississippi*, 21; *Iroquois*, 10 2nd class sloop; *Oneida*, 10; *Verona*, 11; *Cayuga*, 5; *Penola*, 5; *Wissahickon*, 5; *Winona*, 5.

How any controversy could arise as to which branch of the U. S. Service deserves the credit of the capture of New Orleans is a matter of wonder to those who were present at the time. The following article from the Richmond Enquirer of September 10th, 1875, written by an eye-witness of many of the scenes in the city which he describes, would seem conclusively to establish the fact that the navy alone achieved the capture.

The question has again been raised as to whether the army or the navy is entitled to the credit of having captured New Orleans from the Confederates in April or May, 1862. It has been a mooted point in history ever since the event happened, and its discussion has caused no little angry feeling between the two branches of the service. Ben Butler, of course, laid claim to the honours of the capture, and proclaimed himself "the hero" of New Orleans, completely overshadowing Farragut and his fleet, and the lying histories of the day, written in the Radical interest on the other side of the line, have perpetuated the fraud. No citizen of New Orleans who personally knows anything of the circumstances of the fall of the city into the hands of the Federals has ever had any doubts as to who was or is entitled to the credit; but the persistent efforts of Butler and his friends to claim the lion's share in that exploit, have at last called out the Hon. Gideon Welles, Secretary of the Navy in Mr. Lincoln's Cabinet, as the champion of Admiral Farragut and his gallant tars. In the course of an article in the *Hartford Times*, Mr. Welles shows that "In January, 1862, the plan for the reduction of the forts below New Orleans and the capture of the city was fully matured in the Navy Department, Farragut receiving orders in detail for the work on the 20th of that month; that the memorable passage of the forts was made, and the surly submission of the Mayor of New Orleans received by Farragut on the 26th of April, formal possession being immediately taken and the United States flag displayed on the public buildings; that the army was not only absent alike from the plan and the execution of this great movement, but did not appear until May 1, when General Butler's troops arrived, and on the day following entered upon the occupation of the city captured by Farragut.

34

Quite correct, Mr. ex-Secretary. Farragut passed the forts as stated, with the *Hartford* and one or two other vessels, destroyed the ram *Manassas*, and the other Confederate vessels of war, after a most desperate battle, in which at least one of his best ships was sunk, and then made his way in his flag-ship unmolested up the river. He arrived alone in front of New Orleans on the 26th of April, and at noon brought his guns to bear on the city at the head of Girod street. He immediately dispatched Lieutenant Bailey with a flag of truce to the authorities demanding the surrender, and giving them thirty-six hours in which to reply,—at the expiration of which time he should open fire and bombard the place, if an answer favourable to his demand were not received. The city at this time had been partially evacuated by General Lovell and his troops, and all authority had been surrendered by the military to the mayor. The terms submitted by Farragut were discussed for fully twenty-four hours by the Council, assembled at the Mayor's office, and all this time the city was in the hands of a wild, reckless and excited mob of citizens, while people everywhere were flying or preparing for flight, many even in such haste as to leave their houses open and valuables exposed to the depredations of servants or the mob. Perhaps no more fearful scene of confusion was ever witnessed outside of Paris when in the throes of a periodic revolution. It was a novelty then for an American city to be captured or to fall into the hands of an enemy, and the people had some very queer notions about defend-ing it to the last, and fighting the enemy with all sorts of weapons amid its ruins. It was with the utmost difficulty the police could protect Bailey and his middies with their flag of truce. But on the following day, and before the time of grace expired, the Council determined that as they had no means of defence against the enemy's ships, which held the city at the mercy of their guns, it was best to enter into negotiations for the surrender. Farragut then demanded that as a sign of submission the Confederate flag should be hauled down from all points where displayed in the city and replaced by the stars and stripes, and in the meantime he would send a battery with his sailors and marines ashore to maintain order. But no one was found in the city to take the Confederate flags down, and hoist the starry banner in their place; so a battery of ships' guns was landed and hauled through the streets till it reached the City Hall, and there it was placed in position to cover every point of approach. A young middy, apparently about fifteen years of age, then made his appearance at the entrance of the City Hall, bearing a United States flag. He was admitted without opposition, and was shown the way to the top of the building. The lad ascended to the roof, and in full view of an assembled multitude of thousands in the streets and on the housetops, deliberately un-did the halyards and hauled down the Confederate, or rather *Louisiana* state flag; then replacing it with the one he carried, hoisted it to the peak of the staff in its place, and the capture of New Orleans by the navy was complete. Many who witnessed the act of this daring boy trembled for his life, as a rifle shot from any of the houses surrounding, or even from the street, would have proved fatal and put an end to his young life at any moment. So excited was the crowd in the street, when the middy came down, and so fierce the thirst for vengeance upon any object that might present itself, that it was found necessary to hurry him into a close carriage and drive with all speed through back streets, to keep clear of the pressing mob, who, in the blindness of their passion, would perhaps have sacrificed the youngster, had they caught him, to appease their rage.

After this the city began to quiet down. The foreign residents formed themselves into a police and took charge of the streets; and had succeeded pretty well in restoring order, when, on the 2nd of May, Butler landed at the levee from his transports, and marched to the St. Charles, where he established his headquarters and took formal possession of the city. Still he found it no easy matter to subdue the spirit of a people who did not hesitate to jeer at his soldiers or jostle them from the sidewalks as they marched through the streets. But he soon enough became master of the situation, and made the most for himself out of what Farragut had so readily placed in his hands. The navy was certainly entitled to all the credit of the capture; one ship in front of the city with open ports was enough, it did what the entire army of Butler, had it been ten times as numerous, could never have accomplished. New Orleans never would have been taken by the army alone; but the guns of a sloop-of-war in front of an open city are conclusive and irresistible arguments. If it was heroism to capture that city the Confederacy will always be as free to admit that Farragut was the hero of New Orleans, as that Butler was the tyrant, robber, and oppressor of its conquered people.

5. Extract from Commodore Mitchell's official report, dated Aug. 19th, 1862.

During the night of Sunday the 27th we had so far succeeded in operating the propellers that we expected early the next day to make a fair trial of them in connection with the paddle wheels, when at daylight an officer sent by Gen. Duncan came on board to inform us that many of the garrison at Fort Jackson had deserted during the night; that serious disturbances had occurred; and that the disaffection of the men was believed to be general on account of what appeared to them to have become the desperate character of the "defence," etc.

6. Extract from Commodore Mitchell's official report:

I at once returned on board and called a council of war composed of Lieutenants Wilkinson, (commanding) W. H. Ward, A. F. Warley, Wm. C. Whittle, Jr., R. J. Bowen, Arnold, F. M. Harris, and George N. Shryock, by whom—in consequence of the enemy's having the entire command of the river above and below us, with an overwhelming force, and who was in the act of obtaining quiet and undisturbed possession of Forts Jackson and St. Philip, with all their material defences intact, with ordnance, military stores and provisions, thus cutting the *Louisiana* off from all succour or support; and her having on board not more than ten days' provisions, her surrender would be rendered certain in a brief period by the simple method of blockade; and that, in the condition of her motive power and defective steering apparatus, and the immediate danger of attack, she was very liable to capture— it was unanimously recommended that the *Louisiana* be destroyed, forthwith, to prevent her falling into the hands of the enemy, while it remained in our power to prevent it; first retiring to our tenders.

7. The first and only time that I ever saw the notorious General B. F. Butler, who subsequently claimed for himself and the troops under his command, the honour of capturing New Orleans, was on board the *Clifton*. He took passage in her to the city. No one who has ever looked upon that unique countenance can ever forget it; and as his glance rested for a moment upon us, each one conceived himself to be the special object of the General's regard; for owing to his peculiar visual organs, that distinguished individual seems to possess the Argus like faculty of looking steadily at several persons at one and the same time. With the pride that apes humility, or perhaps with the eccentricity of genius, he affected, upon the occasion, a rough costume; wearing a slouch hat, and having his trousers tucked inside of his soiled boots; and he carried in his hand a long stick like a pilgrim's staff. He *preceded* his troops to the city, however, and might therefore, with equal propriety and regard for truth, claim the *sole* glory of its capture.

CHAPTER 4

Prisoner of the Union

On the 9th of May we were transferred from the *Colorado* to the steamer *Rhode Island*, bound to Fort Warren. On board of this vessel we were "tabooed" even more completely by the officers, than on board the *Colorado*; for the *Rhode Island* was officered, with the single exception, I believe, of her captain, by volunteers, who were not connected with us by any associations of friendship or congeniality of taste. The harsh order to hold no intercourse with us, had been evaded or violated, *sub rosa*, on board the *Colorado* by old friends and shipmates. On board the *Rhode Island*, much to our satisfaction, it was strictly obeyed; for we would have lost our patience to be "interviewed" by fledgling naval heroes, many of whom had reached the quarter deck through the hawseholes. Upon one occasion, many years ago, when the question of increasing the United States Navy was under discussion by Congress, a rough western member, opposed to the measure, stated that his section of the country could supply droves of young officers whenever they were needed. The United States Government must have "corralled" lots of youngsters, without regard to their fitness or capacity, to send on board the ships of war during our civil conflict. The "noble commander" of the *Rhode Island* most of us had known of old as a prim little precision, and a great stickler for etiquette, and by no means a bad fellow; but so strict a constructionist that he would probably have refused to recognize his grandfather, if it were against orders. But he had a humane disposition under his frigid exterior; and allowed us all the comfort and privileges compatible with discipline and safety.

We touched at Fortress Monroe; and while the vessel was at anchor there I received a gratifying evidence that this fratricidal war had not destroyed all kindly feelings between former friends and messmates. The executive officer of the *Rhode Island* called me aside to say that a friend wished to see me in his state-room; and as he did not mention the name, I was surprised to find myself warmly greeted by Albert Smith. We had served together during the Mexican war, and our cruise had not been an uneventful one; for the vessel to which we were attached (the *Perry*) after considerable service in the Mexican Gulf, was dismasted and wrecked, during one of the most terrific hurricanes that ever desolated the West India Islands. Thirty-nine vessels, out of forty-two, which lay in the harbour of Havana, foundered at their anchors, or were driven ashore; all of the light-houses along the Florida reef were destroyed, and hundreds of persons perished.

The *Perry* lost all of her boats, her guns, except two, were thrown overboard, and she escaped complete destruction almost by a miracle. She encountered the hurricane off Havana, and after scudding for many hours under bare poles, describing a circle as the wind continued to veer in the cyclone, she passed over the Florida reef with one tremendous shock as she hung for a moment upon its rocky crest. Her masts went by the board, but we had passed in a moment from a raging sea into smooth water. Captain Blake, who commanded her, achieved the feat of rigging jury masts with his crew, and carrying the vessel to the Philadelphia navy yard for repairs. Albert Smith and I had not met for many years. He offered me any service in his power, and pressed me to accept at least a pecuniary loan. The kind offer, although declined, was gratefully remembered; and I was glad, too, to find that he, in common with many others, who remained to fight under the old flag, could appreciate the sacrifices made by those who felt equally bound, by all the truest and best feelings of our nature, to defend their homes and firesides.

On our arrival at Fort Warren we were assigned quarters in one of the casemates. Little more than a year had passed away since I had planted a signal staff upon its parapet to *angle* upon; being then engaged, as chief of a hydrographic surveying party, in surveying the approaches to Boston Harbour. *Then* its garrison consisted of a superannuated sergeant whose office was a sinecure; *now* it held an armed garrison, who drilled and paraded every day, with all the "pomp and circumstance" of war, to the patriotic tune of "John Brown's body lies a-moulding in the grave, but his spirit is marching on;" and it was crowded with southern prisoners of war.

For a few days, in pursuance of Commodore Porter's policy, we were closely confined; but all exceptional restrictions were then removed and we fell into the monotonous routine of prison life. The following correspondence took place previous to the removal of the restrictions, and explains the reason of their withdrawal.

Fort Warren
Boston Harbour
May 25, 1862
Sir,—I was much surprised last evening on being informed by Colonel Dimmick that Lieutenants Wilkinson, Warly, Ward, Whittle and Harris, together with myself, have been, by your order, denied the "privileges and courtesies that are extended to other prisoners," on the ground that the act of burning the Confederate States Battery *Louisiana*, late under my command, was held by the United States Navy Department as "infamous." In my letter to the Department, dated on board of the United States Steamer *Rhode Island*, Key West, May 14th, 1862, and forwarded through Commander Trenchard on the arrival of that vessel in Hampton Roads, together with a copy of my letter to Flag officer

Farragut, and his reply thereto, I felt assured that all the facts connected with the destruction of the *Louisiana* were placed in such a light as not to be mistaken, nor my motives misconstrued. To render the affair still more clear I enclose herewith a memorandum of W. C. Whittle Jr., Confederate States Navy, who was the bearer of my message to Commodore Porter respecting my fears that the magazine of the *Louisiana* had not been effectually drowned. With all these statements forwarded by me to the United States Navy Department I am perfectly willing to rest the case with impartial and unprejudiced minds, as well as with my own Government, satisfied that nothing has been done by the foregoing officers, nor myself, militating at all against the strictest rules of military honour and usage.

Though I will not affect an indifference to the personal annoyance to us by the action of the United States Navy Department in our case as prisoners of war, yet my chief solicitude is to have placed on file in that office such a statement of facts as will, on a fair investigation, vindicate all the officers of the Confederate States Navy concerned from the odium of infamous conduct unjustly attempted to be fixed upon them by those of the United States Navy; against which and the infliction of punishment as directed by the Navy Department I enter my solemn protest.

I most emphatically assert that the *Louisiana*, when abandoned and fired by my order, was not only not "turned adrift" or intended to injure the United States forces as charged by Commander Porter; but that she was actually left secured to the opposite bank of the river and distant quite three-fourths of a mile from the said forces, for the very reason that they were flying a flag of truce, and for that reason I dispatched the warning message to Commander Porter respecting the magazine. That it is not only the right, but the duty, of an officer to destroy public property to prevent its falling into the hands of an enemy does not admit of question; and in addition to all which, it must not be overlooked that the forces under my command flew no flag of truce, and that I was not in any way a party to the surrender of Forts Jackson and St. Philip.

I have the honour to be Very respectfully your obedient servant,
(Signed) *Jno. K. Mitchell*
Commander C. S. Navy

Hon. Gideon Welles
Secretary of the Navy
Washington, D. C.

Copy in Substance
Navy Department
Washington
May 29, 1862
Sir,—The explanations of Commodore J. K. Mitchell are satisfactory, and the restrictions imposed on him and his associates by the department's order of the 2nd instant will be removed, and they will be treated as prisoners of war.

This does not relieve Beverly Kennon from the restrictions imposed on him.
(Signed) *Gideon Welles*

Colonel Justin Dimmick
Commanding Fort Warren
Boston

Copy
Navy Department
June 25, 1862
Sir,—The letter of John K. Mitchell of the 20th inst., concerning the restrictions imposed on you, by order of this Department, at Fort Warren, has been received.

Will you please furnish the Department with the

particulars of the destruction of the gunboat of which you had command in the engagement below New Orleans, with wounded men on board.

I am respectfully your obedient servant,
(Signed) *Gideon Welles*

Beverly Kennon
Fort Warren
Boston

Copy
Fort Warren
Boston
June 28, 1862

Hon. Gideon Welles
Secretary U. S. Navy

Sir,—Colonel Dimmick, the commander of this post, delivered to me yesterday a letter signed by you under date of June 25th directed to me as "Beverly Kennon" and referring to a communication addressed to you on the 20th inst. by my superior officer, Commander J. K. Mitchell, of the Confederate States Navy, whom you are pleased to designate as "John K. Mitchell."

The purport of your letter is a request that I will furnish your Department of the United States Government with the "particulars of the destruction of the gunboat of which I had command in the engagement below New Orleans with wounded men on board."

When I destroyed and left the vessel which I had commanded on the occasion referred to, all the wounded men had been removed, the most of them lowered into boats by my own hands. I was, myself, the last person to leave the vessel. Any statements which you may have received to the contrary are wholly without foundation. It would not be proper, under any circumstances, that I should report to you the "particulars" of her destruction; that being a matter which concerns my own Government exclusively, and with which yours can have nothing to do. Should any charges be made against me, however, of which you have a right to take cognizance under the laws of war, I will with pleasure, respond to any respectful communication which you may address me on the subject. Indeed I shall be glad of the opportunity to vindicate my character as an officer from the unjust and unfounded imputations which have been cast upon it in the connection to which you allude, and upon the faith of which I have already been disparaged by unusual restrictions and confinements, here and elsewhere, since I have been a prisoner of war, without having been furnished an opportunity for such vindication. But your letter of the 20th inst. so studiously denies, both to Commander Mitchell and myself, not only our official designations, but those of common courtesy, that while I am unwilling to believe you would intentionally offer an indignity to prisoners of war in your power, I can not now make further reply without failing in respect to myself as well as to my superior officer and Government.

I am Sir, very respectfully, your obedient servant,

(Signed) *Beverly Kennon*,

Commander in Provisional Navy of the state of Louisiana in the Confederate service

The restrictions were removed from Kennon in a few days after the close of this correspondence.

Many distinguished political prisoners were at that time confined at Fort Warren; and all of the officers captured at Fort Donelson. Among the former class, were those members of the Maryland Legislature, and of the Baltimore City Council, who had been arrested and imprisoned by the United States Government for alleged treason. It was my good fortune to be invited into this mess. It is not my purpose to inflict upon the reader a detailed account of prison life during the war, which has been described by far abler pens than mine.

All the members of our mess took their turns, either at carving or waiting upon the table, and guests were never better served. The graceful and accomplished old Commodore B. and General T. shone conspicuous as carvers; while Colonels, Majors and Captains, with spotless napkins on their arms, anticipated every wish of the guests at the table. Colonel Dimmick was honoured and beloved by the prisoners for his humanity, and he and his family will ever be held in affectionate remembrance by them; many of us having received special acts of kindness, while suffering from sickness. When his son was ordered to active service in the field I believe there was an unanimous prayer by the prisoners that his life would be spared through the perils he was about to encounter.

The prisoners, first giving their parole not to attempt to escape, were allowed the range of nearly the whole island during the day; and not infrequently suffered to see relatives and friends who had received permission from the proper authorities to visit them. In happier *ante bellum* times, I had known some of the good people of Boston, and had spent a portion of a summer with several families at that pleasant watering place, Nahant.

One of my most esteemed friends—Mrs. L— with the charity of a noble and Christian heart, wrote to me as soon as she learned that I was a prisoner; but she was too loyal to the flag not to express regret and distress at what she believed to be a mistaken sense of duty. The reader may remember the definition once given of "Orthodoxy" by a dignitary of the church of England to an inquiring nobleman. "Orthodoxy, my Lord, is *my* doxy, heterodoxy is *your* doxy if you differ from me." The same authority, it has always appeared to me, was assumed by a large portion of the Northern people. They demanded a Government to suit their ideas, and disloyalty consisted in opposing them.

We were permitted to write once a month to our friends in the Confederacy; the letters being left open for inspection. There were a few Northerners among us, but I know of only a single case where the individual concerned so far yielded to the persuasion of his friends outside, as to renounce the cause which he had sworn to defend.

Aside from the confinement, and the earnest desire to be doing our part in the war, there could be no cause to repine at our lot. We were allowed, at our own expense, to supply our tables from the Boston market, not only abundantly, but luxuriously; the Government furnishing the usual rations; and the prisoners grew robust upon the good fare and the bracing climate. A tug plied daily between Boston and the island on which Fort Warren is situated. We were permitted to receive the daily papers and to purchase clothing and other necessaries, either from the sutler, or from outside; and many of the prisoners were indebted to a noble charity for the means of supplying many of these needs; of clothing especially, which was chiefly furnished by the firm of Noah Walker & Co. of Baltimore. The firm itself was said to be most liberal, not merely dispensing the donations received in Baltimore and elsewhere, but supplying a large amount of clothing gratuitously.

The policy of retaliation had not then been adopted. It is conceded that the United States Government, towards the close of the war, subjected the Confederate prisoners in their hands to harsh treatment in pursuance of this policy; but in justice to the Confederate authorities it should be borne in mind that they repeatedly proposed an exchange of prisoners upon the ground of humanity, seeing that neither provisions nor medicine were procurable; and, I believe, it is also a conceded fact that General Grant opposed exchanges. The testimony of General *Lee* given before the "reconstruction" Committee, clearly establishes the fact that *he* did all in his power to effect this object. In answer to a question he says: "I offered to General Grant around Richmond that we should ourselves exchange all the prisoners in our hands, and to show that I would do whatever was in my power, I offered them to send to City

Point all the prisoners in Virginia and North Carolina, over which my command extended, providing they returned an equal number of mine, man for man. I reported this to the War Department, and received for answer, that they would place at my command all the prisoners at the South, if the proposition was accepted." The Rev. J. Wm. Jones, D.D., author of *Personal Reminiscences of General R. E. Lee*, writes as follows upon this subject *viz*:

1st—The Confederate authorities gave to prisoners in their hands the same rations which they issued to their own soldiers, and gave them the very best accommodations which their scant means afforded.

2nd. They were always anxious to exchange prisoners, man for man, and when this was rejected by the Federal authorities, they offered to send home the prisoners in their hands without any equivalent.

3rd. By refusing all propositions to exchange prisoners, and declining even to receive their own men without equivalent the Federal authorities made themselves responsible for all the suffering, of both Federal and Confederate prisoners, that ensued.

4th. And yet notwithstanding these facts, it is susceptible of proof, from the official records of the Federal Department, that the suffering of Confederate prisoners in Federal prisons was much greater than that of Federal prisoners in Confederate prisons. Without going more fully into the question, the following figures, from the report of Mr. Stanton, Secretary of War, in response to a resolution of the House of Representatives, calling for the number of prisoners on both sides and their mortality, are triumphantly submitted.

	In prison	Died
U. S. Soldiers	260,940	22,526
Confederates	200,000	26,500

That is, the Confederate States held as prisoners nearly 61,000 more men than the Federals; and yet the death of Federal prisoners fell below those of the Confederates four thousand.

Lastly, the Southern Historical Society, Richmond, Va., has recently published *A Vindication of the Confederacy Against the Charge of Cruelty to Prisoners*, which is conclusive on the whole question. It was compiled by the Secretary of the Society, the Rev. J. Wm. Jones, just quoted, who concludes with the following summing up of his argument.

We think that we have established the following points:

1st. The laws of the Confederate Congress, the orders of the War Department, the Regulations of the Surgeon General, the action of our Generals in the field, and the orders of those who had the immediate charge of the prisoners, all provided that prisoners in the hands of the Confederates should be kindly treated, supplied with the same rations which our soldiers had, and cared for, when sick, in hospitals placed on *precisely the same footing as the hospitals for Confederate soldiers.*

2nd. If these regulations were violated in individual instances, and if subordinates were sometimes cruel to prisoners, it was without the knowledge or consent of the Confederate Government, which always took prompt action on any case reported to them.

3rd. If the prisoners failed to get their full rations, and had those of inferior quality, the Confederate soldiers suffered in precisely the same way and to the same extent; and it resulted from that system of warfare adopted by the Federal authorities, which carried desolation and ruin to every part of the South they could reach, and which in starving the Confederates into submission, brought the same evils upon their own men in Southern prisons.

4th. The mortality in Southern prisons (fearfully large, although over three per cent less than the mortality in Northern prisons) resulted from causes beyond the control of our authorities, from epidemics, etc., which might have been avoided or greatly mitigated had not the Federal Government declared medicines "contraband of war," refused the proposition of Judge Ould, that each Government should send its own surgeons with medicines, hospital stores, etc., to minister to soldiers in prison, declined his proposition to send medicines to its own men in southern prisons, without being required to allow the Confederates the same privileges—refused to allow the Confederate Government to buy medicines for gold, tobacco, or cotton, which it offered to pledge its honour should be used only for Federal prisoners in its hands, refused to exchange sick and wounded, and neglected from August to December, 1864, to accede to Judge Ould's proposition to send transportation to Savannah and receive *without equivalent* from ten to fifteen thousand Federal prisoners, notwithstanding the fact that this offer was accompanied with a statement of the utter inability of the Confederacy to provide for these prisoners, and a detailed report of the monthly mortality at Andersonville, and that Judge Ould, again and again, urged compliance with his humane proposal.

5th. We have proven by the most unimpeachable testimony, that the sufferings of Confederate prisoners in Northern "prison pens," were terrible beyond description; that they were starved in a land of plenty, that they were frozen where fuel and clothing were abundant; that they suffered untold horrors for want of medicines, hospital stores and proper medical attention; that they were shot by sentinels, beaten by officers, and subjected to the most cruel punishments upon the slightest pretexts; that friends at the North were refused the privilege of clothing their nakedness or feeding them when starving; and that these outrages were perpetrated not only with the full knowledge of, but under the orders of E. M. Stanton, United States Secretary of War. We have proven these things by Federal as well as Confederate testimony.

6th. We have shown that all the suffering of prisoners on both sides could have been avoided by simply carrying out the terms of the cartel, and that for the failure to do this, the *Federal authorities alone* were responsible; that the Confederate Government originally proposed the cartel, and were always ready to carry it out both in letter and spirit; that the Federal authorities observed its terms only so long as it was to their interest to do so, and then repudiated their plighted faith and proposed other terms which were greatly to the disadvantage of the Confederates; that when the Government at Richmond agreed to accept the hard terms of exchange offered them, these were at once repudiated by the Federal authorities; that when Judge Ould agreed upon a new cartel with General Butler, Lieutenant-General Grant refused to approve it, and Mr. Stanton repudiated it; and that the policy of the Federal Government was to refuse all exchanges while they "fired the Northern heart" by placing the whole blame upon the "Rebels," and by circulating the most heartrending stories of "Rebel barbarity" to prisoners. If either of the above points has not been made clear to any sincere seeker after the truth, we would be most happy to produce further testimony. And we hold ourselves prepared to maintain against all comers, the *truth of every proposition we have laid down in this discussion.* Let the calm verdict of history decide between the Confederate Government and its calumniators.

These extracts are inserted with the hope that the fair minded reader may be induced to read the evidence upon the Confederate side.

It is not to be denied that the sufferings in Confederate prisons were fearful; but they were caused by the destitute condition of the country ravaged by war, and the scarcity of medicines which were not to be obtained.

We were growing very tired of the monotony of prison life, scarcely varied except by the daily game of football and the semi-weekly reports of the capture of Richmond, when a rumour began to circulate of a speedy exchange of prisoners. It was about the time when General McClellan "changed his base" from the lines around Richmond to Harrison's Landing, on James River. Early in August a large number of us, military and naval officers, were sent on board a transport bound to James River, where we arrived in due time, and thence, after taking on board a number of Confederates forwarded from other prisons, we proceeded up the river to Aiken's Landing. There was fighting near Malvern Hill as we passed by there, and the United States gunboats had been shelling the Confederate troops. The crew of one of them was at quarters, the men in their snow white "frocks" and trousers, the beautifully polished eight inch guns cast loose and ready for action.

The captain of one of the guns, a handsome man-of-war's man, looked at our party with a smile of bravado as we passed by, at the same time tapping his gun with his hand. Garrick or Kean could not have conveyed more meaning by a gesture. That handsome fellow's confidence in his pet was not misplaced; for history records how frequently during the war the tide of battle was turned by that gallant Navy to which it is an honour ever to have belonged. We, who so reluctantly severed our connection with it, still feel a pride in its achievements; and in our dreams are frequently pacing the deck, or sitting at the mess table with dear friends of "auld lang syne," from whom we are probably severed forever on this side of eternity.

We were put ashore at Aiken's Landing on the 5th of August. It was a hot, sultry day. Three or four poor fellows had died on board our transport while on our way up the river, and their bodies were landed at the same time with ourselves. While we were waiting for the preliminaries for the exchange of prisoners to be settled between the Commissioners, a large grave was dug in the sand with such implements as could be procured, and the "unknown" were consigned to their last resting place between high and low water mark.

CHAPTER 5

Exchanged

After reporting at the Navy Department, I proceeded to
my home. The day after my arrival there I was summoned by
telegram to Richmond, to report in person to the Secretary
of War. I had been detailed for special duty, and from this date
commenced my connection with blockade running. Upon
reaching the office, I found written instructions from the Secretary of War to proceed to England and purchase a steamer
suitable for running the blockade, to load her with arms, munitions of war, and other supplies, and to bring her into a
Confederate port with all dispatch. Ample funds in sterling
exchange were provided and a large amount of Confederate
bonds was entrusted to me for deposit with an agent of the
Government in England.

Accompanied by my small staff of assistants, and by Major Ben. Ficklin, who went abroad under special instructions
from the War and Treasury Departments, I left Richmond
about the 12th of August, and after some difficulty and delay,
secured passage for the whole party on board the little steamer *Kate*, about to sail from Wilmington for Nassau. Under her
skilful commander, Lockwood, this little side-wheel steamer
had already acquired fame as a successful blockade-runner,
and was destined to continue successful to the end of her
career. But her appearance was by no means prepossessing,
and she was very slow, her maximum speed being about nine
knots. I forget by what accident she was at last disabled; per-

haps by sheer old age and infirmity; but her ribs were to be seen for many a day before the war ended, bleaching in the sun on one of the mud flats in Cape Fear River.

The night of our crossing the bar was dark and stormy and we felt under great obligations to the blockading fleet outside, for showing lights at their peaks—thus enabling us to avoid them with much ease. At this period, indeed, blockade running had not assumed such enormous proportions as it afterwards attained, when hundreds of thousands of dollars were invested in a single venture and the profits were so immense that the game was well worth the candle. Subsequent to the period of which I now write, Wilmington became the chief place of import and export. Large quantities of cotton were stored there, both on Government and private account; and steam cotton presses were erected, but at this period Charleston possessed greater facilities and was perhaps quite as accessible.

Our voyage to Nassau was safely accomplished; the vigilant look-out at the mast-head giving prompt notice of a speck on the horizon no larger than a gull's wing, when the course would be so changed as to lose sight of it. Two cases of yellow fever, both ending fatally, occurred among the passengers during the brief voyage, and we were quarantined on our arrival at Nassau. One of the sick men had been brought on deck and placed on a couch under the deck awning. As he had taken no nourishment for two or three days, our good captain directed that a bowl of soup should be prepared for him. The sick man sat up when the steaming bowl was presented to him; seized it with both hands, drained it to the bottom, and fell back dead. We had not been at anchor more than an hour when an outward-bound passing schooner hailed us and announced to our captain the death of his wife and child, whom he had left in good health only a few days before.

As the epidemic on board the *Kate* had been contracted at Nassau, and still prevailed on shore, we were at a loss to understand why we should be refused *pratique*; but it gave our little party no concern, as the town did not present an attractive or inviting appearance from the quarantine ground; nor were our unfavourable impressions removed upon a nearer acquaintance with it two or three months afterwards. But it was evident, that in spite of the epidemic, there was a vast deal of activity ashore and afloat. Cotton, cotton, everywhere!

Blockade-runners discharging it into lighters, tier upon tier of it, piled high upon the wharves, and merchant vessels, chiefly under the British flag, loading with it. Here and there in the crowded harbour might be seen a long, low, rakish-looking lead-coloured steamer with short masts, and a convex forecastle deck extending nearly as far aft as the waist, and placed there to enable the steamer to be forced *through* and not *over* a heavy head sea. These were the genuine blockade-runners, built for speed; and some of them survived all the desperate hazards of the war.

The mulatto undertaker, who came on board to take the measure for coffins for the two passengers who had died, did not leave us in a very cheerful state of mind, although *he* was in fine spirits, in the anticipation of a brisk demand for his stock in trade.

Presenting each one of us with his card, he politely expressed the hope that we would give him our custom, if we needed anything in his line. Fortunately we had no occasion for his services. Just before leaving the ship he was invited to take a glass of brandy and water. Holding the glass in his hands which were yet stained with the coffin paint, he drank to our death, a toast to which Dyer, my Wilmington pilot, responded, "You shouldn't bury me, you d——d rascal, if I *did* die."

With the assistance of the Confederate agent on shore, we succeeded in promptly chartering a schooner for Cardenas and in provisioning her for the voyage; and in a day or two, were making our way across the Bahama Banks for Cuba. The agent had supplied us liberally with flesh, fowls, and ice; and the Banks gave us an abundance of fish, as the light winds fanned us slowly along, sometimes freshening into a moderate breeze, and occasionally dying away to a calm. The *"chef d'oeuvre"* of our mulatto skipper who was also cook, was conch soup, and he was not only an adept at cooking but also at catching the conch. In those almost transparent waters, the smallest object can be distinctly seen at the depth of three or four fathoms. When soup was to be prepared Captain Dick would take his station at the bow *in puris naturalibus*, watching intently for his prize. Overboard he would go like an arrow, and rising again to the surface, would pitch the conch (and sometimes one in each hand) on board. His son Napoleon Bonaparte, (who was first mate, steward and half the starboard watch) would throw him a rope, and the old fellow would climb on board as the little craft sailed by, without an alteration in her course.

Major Ben. Ficklin was attacked with yellow fever just after we left Nassau; but as we had no medicines on board he recovered. The medical fraternity might perhaps take a hint from the treatment of his case. Small lumps of ice were kept in a saucer beside him as he lay on a mattress under a deck awning, and by the constant use of it he allayed the raging thirst attending high fever. The *vis medicatrix naturæ* accomplished the rest.

Having no books on board, we beguiled the time occasionally by telling stories as we lay under the shelter of the deck awning. One of my contributions was the following:

Many officers of the navy will remember it, and there are some who, like myself, will recollect the solemn earnestness with which the hero of it would narrate the facts, for he firmly believed it to the day of his death. At the time of its occurrence he was enjoying a day's shooting at his home in Vermont. Becoming tired toward midday he took a seat on an old log in the woods. A few minutes afterwards, he saw an old bareheaded man, meanly clad, approaching, who seated himself in silence at the other end of the log. The head of the stranger was bound with a white cloth and his eyes were fixed with a glassy stare upon Major B., who felt his blood run cold at the singular apparition. At last the Major mustered up courage to ask the stranger what he wanted. The spectre replied:

"I am a dead man, and was buried in the graveyard yonder" (pointing as he spoke to a dilapidated enclosure a few yards distant). "The dogs," he continued, "have found their way into my shallow grave, and are gnawing my flesh. I can not rest until I am laid deeper in the ground."

The Major used to assert that his tongue clove to the roof of his mouth; but he managed to promise the dead man that his wishes should be complied with, when the apparition dissolved into the air. The Major went straight to some of the neighbours, and when he accompanied them to the grave, it was found in the condition described by its occupant. N. B. The Major was in the habit of carrying a "pocket pistol," which may have been overcharged upon this occasion; he *also* belonged to the *marines*.

We arrived at Cardenas after a week's voyage, and stopped there a day to recruit. During our stay we witnessed a curious scene. While we were enjoying our cigars in the cool of the evening upon the *azotea* of our hotel, we saw a file of soldiers march up to a house directly opposite, and after repeated efforts to enter, they finally burst open the door; reappearing in a few moments with seven or eight "coolies," who were apparently dead drunk, but in reality were stupefied with opium; having met, by appointment, to "shuffle off this mortal coil" after this characteristic fashion. One or two of them were quite beyond resuscitation, and the others were only prevented from sinking into fatal insensibility by severe flogging with bamboo canes, and being forced to keep upon their feet. We were informed that suicide is very common among them in Cuba; it being their last resort against misery and oppression.

Colonel Totten, the able civil engineer who constructed the railroad across the Isthmus of Panama, once gave a party of us a graphic account of the mortality among a number of them, who had been employed by him in that pestilential climate. Having no access to opium, and being deprived of knives, they resorted to the most ingenious modes of self destruction. Sometimes they would wade out in the bay at low water, with a pole, which they would stick firmly into the mud, and securely tying themselves to it, would wait for the rising tide to drown them. Others would point a stake by charring it in the fire and impale themselves upon it.

The evils of this system of labour cannot be truthfully denied. Ignorant even of the nature of the contract which binds them to servitude, the coolies are driven in crowds to the ship which is to transport them to another hemisphere; and they endure all the horrors of the "middle passage" during their long voyage.

When they arrive at their port of destination in the West Indies they are apprenticed for a term of years to the planters who need their services, and many of them succumb to the tropical climate and the severe labour in the cane field. Many more seek a ready means of escape in death. The philanthropy of the civilized governments, which has been concentrated for many years upon efforts to liberate the "black man and brother," has never been exerted to rescue "John Chinaman" from a crueller thraldom and a harder lot.

Taking the train for Havana, we passed through a very beautiful country, luxuriant with tropical verdure; the most conspicuous natural feature in the landscape being the graceful palm tree in its many varieties. We passed, too, many sugar plantations, the growing cane not at all unlike our own cornfields at home, while the long lines of negroes, at work with their hoes, in the crop, made the fields appear even more familiar and home-like. Our friends, the "darkies," evidently did not contemplate suicide. Sleek and well-fed, they were chattering like so many flocks of blackbirds.

Arriving at Havana we took up our quarters at Mrs. B.'s hotel, and as my first object was to find Colonel Helm, the agent of the Confederate Government, I started for that purpose immediately after our arrival.

The Colonel had held the position of United States Consul before the war; and the residence then occupied by him was now tenanted by his successor. Being directed to this house by mistake, I was ushered in by the servant, and found myself face to face with Captain S., the American Consul. We were not totally unacquainted, having met occasionally in bygone days, when both of us were in the United States Navy. The surprise was mutual, and the awkward silence was interrupted by my saying "Apparently I am in the wrong pew."

"Evidently," he replied, and we parted without another word.

With the assistance of Colonel Helm our business in Havana was speedily transacted; and passage was engaged for the whole party on board a Spanish steamer bound for St. Thomas, thence to take passage by the British mail steamer for Southampton.

The few days spent in Havana were pleasantly passed in sight-seeing; the afternoons being devoted to a ride upon the *paseo*, and the evenings closed by a visit to the noted Dominica, the principal café of the city. There are many beautiful rides and drives in the environs, and the summer heats are tempered by the cool refreshing sea breeze which blows daily. That scourge of the tropics, yellow fever, is chiefly confined to the cities of Cuba, the country being salubrious; and it appears strange that this beautiful island has never been a favourite place of resort, during the winter, for invalids from the Northern States in search of an equable climate.

It must be confessed that Havana itself possesses few attractions for the stranger and that its sanitary arrangements are execrable. In addition to the imperfect municipal regulations in this respect, all the sewage of the city empties itself into the harbour, in which there is no current to sweep the decomposing matter into the Gulf Stream outside. The water in the harbour is sometimes so phosphorescent at night that showers of liquid fire appear to drop from a boat's oars passing through it; and the boat leaves a long lane of light in her wake.

No stranger visiting Havana fails to see the spot in the cathedral held sacred as the tomb of Columbus. His remains were transferred here with great pomp, after resting many years in the city of San Domingo, whither they had been carried from Spain.

The fish market and the Tacon theatre too, are well worth a visit. Both of them once belonged to the same individual, the noted pirate Marti, whom I have seen many a time, in the streets of Havana, after his reformation. He was then a venerable looking old gentleman. For a long time he had been chief of all the piratical bands that then infested the shores of Cuba. They plied their fearful trade with comparative impunity; the numerous lagoons on the coast, only accessible through tortuous and shallow channels, and hidden by mangrove bushes, affording safe shelter; while they could easily intercept many vessels passing through the narrow strait separating Cuba from Florida. They gave no quarter to man, woman, or child, and scuttled their prizes after taking from them what was most valuable.

A ready sale was found for their plunder in Havana through accomplices there; and their depredations upon commerce finally became so extensive that the United States Government fitted out an expedition against them. General Tacon, at that time Governor-General of Cuba, also prepared an expedition to operate against them. This fleet was on the eve of sailing. The night was dark and rainy. A stranger, wrapped in a cloak for disguise, watched the sentry on duty before the door of the palace from a hiding place near by; and as the sentry turned his back for a moment or two from the door, the stranger slipped by him, undiscovered, and proceeded rapidly to the apartments of the Captain-General. His Excellency was writing at a table; and the stranger had opened the door and entered the room without being discovered. When the Governor-General raised his eyes and saw the cloaked figure standing silently before him, he stretched his hand toward a bell near him, but the stranger interposed.

"Stop, your Excellency," he said, "I am here upon a desperate enterprise. I have come to deliver into your hands every pirate on the Cuban coast upon one condition; a pardon for myself."

"You shall have it," replied His Excellency, "but who are you?"

"I am Marti, and I rely upon the promise you have given to me."

The Governor-General repeated his assurances of immunity upon the prescribed conditions. Marti had laid his plans well, having appointed a place of rendezvous for the different bands before venturing upon his perilous expedition. He acted as a guide to the force sent in pursuit, and every pirate was captured and afterwards *garrotted*. A large price had been set upon the head of Marti. This is the story as told by his contemporaries. For these distinguished services to the state the vile old reprobate was offered the promised reward. In lieu of it he asked for the monopoly of the sale of fish in Havana, which was granted to him; and the structure erected by him for a fish market is perhaps the finest of the sort in the world. He afterwards built the noble Tacon theatre, named after his benefactor—and died in the odour of sanctity.

We were not sorry when the day of our departure came. There was a motley crowd of passengers on board the little steamer. *Paisanos* wearing broad brimmed sombreros and in picturesque costume; *Padres* in their long gowns and shovel hats; pretty *senoritas* with hair plaited down their backs, and officers on their way to join the army in the field in San Domingo. But every one was amiable and disposed to be companionable. Most of them were aware of the fact that there was a state of war between the North and the South; and their sympathies were altogether with our side; for no earthly reason, probably, except that they entertained the blind hatred against the *Norte Americanos* so prevalent among the Latin race on this continent, and supposed the people of the South to be of different origin.[8]

We were half poisoned, and wholly saturated with garlic, while on board the little steamer; and men, women and children smoked incessantly. Our clever artist, Johnny T., drew a capital sketch of a portly old lady whose habit it was, after every meal, to take from her side pocket an oilskin bundle of huge cigars—evidently *plantations*, and made to order. Selecting one, she would strike a light with her *matchero* and begin to puff away like a furnace. When fairly alight, she would dispose of the smoke in some mysterious inner receptacle, whence it would issue in a minute or more, from nose, eyes, ears, and even through the pores of her mahogany-coloured skin, as it appeared to us.

We touched at many little ports, all of them very pretty and picturesque; little quiet basins of blue water, with the houses scattered about along the hill sides, and half hidden by foliage; the white surf thundering outside, and the surface, inside, glassy smooth. Our last port in Cuba was Santiago, since made memorable as the scene of the murder of the gallant and unfortunate Fry, and his companions in misfortune. Should these lines ever meet the eye of any of his old friends and comrades in the United States Navy, they will bear witness, that a brave and noble gentleman was there cruelly done to death. He had lost everything by our war, and dire poverty, with the responsibility of a family to support, forced him to the desperate venture of running the blockade in Cuba. *Morally* he was not more criminal than the British naval officers, who engaged in the same hazardous pursuit during our struggle.

NOTES

8. The educated Cubans must be exonerated from this charge. Many of this class have been at the schools and colleges in the United States; and admire our republican institutions. They are even now, and have been for years, maintaining a desperate struggle for the establishment of these institutions among themselves.

CHAPTER 6

To England

We touched at the little port of San Domingo in the island of Dominica on our way to St. Thomas; and lay at anchor there long enough to allow the passengers to visit the shore for a few hours.

It was once a prosperous town, but is now in ruins, and hovels stand upon the very sites where once arose magnificent palaces; for it was at one time the chief seat of the Spanish Empire in the New World, and the place of residence of Columbus himself. Cortez, the Conqueror of Mexico, once lived in its vicinity. The cathedral still stands entire and is still used as a place of worship, but the walls of the convent attached to the cathedral have yielded to the corroding influences of time and the climate, and are crumbling into ruins. The palace of Diego Columbus, the son of the immortal admiral, who to Castile and Leon gave a new world, is still pointed out, but that, too, is a mere shell, the roof having entirely disappeared.

The population is a wretched mongrel indolent race, and there is little to do there. The whole island, indeed, long ago fell from its high estate, and everywhere thorns and brambles grow where once there were well cultivated plantations. I had previously visited many portions of the island, and saw wherever I went, the same evidences of misrule and indolence; but, the negroes, who hold the western portion of it or Haiti, are physically, at least, a finer race of people than the degenerate, puny hybrids of the eastern part, who have *miscegenated* to an extent that would satisfy the most enthusiastic admirer of our sable "friends and fellow-citizens."

I have never seen finer specimens of stalwart manhood than in Solouque's army years ago, although the *tout ensemble* of it was sufficiently ludicrous; the officers being mounted on ponies a little bigger than goats; and some of them wearing no apparel, except a coat and cocked hat; with spurs on their naked heels; and the ragged half-naked privates chewing one end of a big stick of sugar cane (their only rations) as they marched. Upon one occasion, an officer of the ship to which I was attached, had died at sea, and was buried at Gonaives, with military honours.

The drummer and fifer of our guard of marines were little fellows of twelve or thirteen years of age. The black military commandant of the district was so captivated with their appearance, as they marched at the head of the funeral procession, that he *corralled* all the little *niggers* within his district the next day, to select from them a few drummers and fifers; and I believe there would have been a *casus belli* if our little musicians had been sent ashore, for I doubt if he could have resisted the temptation to kidnap them.

We arrived at St. Thomas two days before the mail-steamer was due and took up our quarters at the only hotel of which the town boasted, but it was an excellent one. The black steward, who superintended the staff of waiters, was a noticeable personage, speaking several languages with correctness and fluency. We appreciated the *cuisine* of the hotel, after so long a diet upon garlic and rancid sweet oil; and were content to pass the greater part of the time at the Ice House, a refreshment saloon conducted by a Vermont "Yankee," but who had been so long abroad as to have become cosmopolitan in his ideas and opinions.

The residence of General Santa Anna, the old Mexican hero, then in exile, was pointed out to us; a handsome building crowning a hill overlooking the town; and we were informed that the old gentleman was still passionately fond of his favourite amusement, cock-fighting.

We sailed for Southampton in the British mail steamer *Atrato*, the best appointed and most comfortable ship on board which I have ever taken passage. She was a paddle-wheel steamer of the first class, belonging to the Cunards, who boast that not a life or a mail has ever been lost in their line. There was a very good band of musicians on board, and the weather during the whole voyage was so pleasant that dancing could be enjoyed. The screw steamers, now so rapidly superseding the old "side wheelers," possess many advantages, it is true, but the superior comfort of the passengers is not to be reckoned among them.

Arriving at Southampton, we took the first train for London. What specially attracted the admiration of our little party as the train sped along, was the exquisite beauty of the country. Almost every view would have furnished a subject for a landscape painter. We saw vast lawns green as emeralds, with clumps of fine trees here and there, and dotted with cattle and sheep; and would frequently catch a glimpse of castles and country seats beautifully ornamented with parks and gardens. It was a series of pictures of rural repose and quiet, embellished with perfect taste. Even the thatched cottages, with their trim hedges, their little flower gardens, and the vines covering the outside, were most picturesque. What a striking contrast with the log cabins and "snake" fences in our own loved "Dixie!"

The Secretary of War, in his instructions to me, had stated that Major Ficklin, who had lately returned from Europe, had been struck by the qualities of a steamer which, in the Major's opinion, was admirably adapted for blockade-running. She was called the *Giraffe*, a Clyde built iron steamer, and plied as a packet between Glasgow and Belfast. She was a side-wheel of light draft, very strongly built and reputed to be of great speed. She possessed the last quality, it is true, but not to such a degree as represented, for her best rate of speed while under my command never exceeded thirteen and a half knots.

Under the same instructions I was to examine the ship and if the inspection proved favourable, the Major was to negotiate for the purchase. I have always believed that some informal arrangement had been made between the parties concerned during the Major's late visit to England. However that may have been, we found, on our arrival in London that the *Giraffe* had been sold within a day or two, to a company about to engage in blockade-running. The manager of this company was Mr. Alexander Collie, who subsequently made such immense ventures, and became so well known in connection with blockade-running.

The Major did not lose heart upon learning that the *Giraffe* had changed hands, but all his efforts to get possession of the vessel were unsuccessful, Mr. C. refusing to part with her upon any terms. As a last resort the Major, whose resources were almost inexhaustible, suggested that I should make an effort. All difficulties instantly vanished, when I informed Mr. Collie that I held a commission in the Confederate States Navy, and had been sent abroad to buy a ship for the Confederate Government. He instantly agreed to transfer possession for the amount paid by him, £32,000, stipulating, however, that the steamer should not be sold, during the war, to private parties without the consent of the company represented by him, who were to have the refusal of her. Although these conditions conflicted with certain arrangements made between the Confederate Secretary of War and Major Ficklin, the latter assented to them; and the *Giraffe* became the property of the Confederate States Government.

The necessary alterations to fit her for a blockade-runner were at once commenced. Her beautiful saloon and cabins were dismantled and bulkheads constructed to separate the quarters for officers and men from the space to be used for stowage of a cargo. Purchases of arms, clothing, etc., were to be made; and after much disgust and vexation of spirit, I employed Mr. Collie, who was a shrewd and practical man of business, to make the purchases on commission, while I found more congenial employment. Long afterwards, when I got a friend in Richmond to prepare my accounts for the auditor, he proved conclusively from the vouchers (which I was careful to preserve) that the Confederate Government owed me £1,000; but I never applied for the "little balance" and now it is buried with the "lost cause."

The Hon. J. M. Mason, representing the Confederate Government, was living very quietly and unostentatiously in London; and although not officially recognized, he was the frequent guest of the nobility and gentry of the kingdom. He looked, so I thought, the equal of any peer in the land, for he was of a noble presence; and he possessed that rare tact of adapting himself to almost any company in which he might be thrown. We always met with a cordial welcome from him; and it was very interesting to hear his comments upon the government and the social life of England. I am sure the contrast between the conservatism, stability and respect for precedents and laws, so manifest everywhere in that favoured land, and the rapidly growing disregard of all these obligations in our own country, struck him most forcibly. He closed a long eulogy of England upon one occasion by remarking, "This is the best Government upon the earth—*except of course our own.*"

He, in common with others, who had access to private sources of information, believed, at that time, that the Confederacy would soon be recognized by England and France; and it appears from evidence made public since the close of the war, that their hopes were by no means groundless; the Emperor of the French having proposed joint recognition to the British government; but all efforts in that direction were thwarted by the "Exeter Hall" influence.

We saw of course many of the sights and curiosities of London. One pleasant day of leisure, after a walk to see that magnificent pile, the Houses of Parliament, I was sauntering along, without thought of where I was going, until I found myself in a perfect labyrinth of filthy streets and tumble down buildings and presenting all the other evidences of vice and poverty; the very neighbourhood in short of "Tom Allalone's" lair. Fortunately I met a policeman who guided me into a respectable part of the city. He told me that I was about to invade the worst section of London, almost within a stone's throw of the Houses of Parliament.

It is astonishing how frequently Dickens' characters and descriptions come into the memory of a stranger visiting London. No one, who has ever seen them, will forget the houses in Chancery. Situated as some of them are, in the busiest and most crowded parts of the city, and mouldering away from disuse and neglect, the idea constantly presented itself to me as I passed one of them, "there is more of the Jarndyce property," and I never saw an "old clo'" man that the rascally Fagin and his hopeful *protégés* did not rise to my recollection. How wonderful is the power of genius which can not only "give to airy nothings a local habitation and a name," but fix them as realities in our memory forever!

At that period the credit of the Confederate Government abroad was excellent; and either from love of "filthy lucre" or of the cause, some of the best firms in England were ready and eager to furnish supplies. It appeared quite practicable to send in machinery, iron plates, etc., for building small vessels of war; and several firms offered to engage in the enterprise, receiving Confederate bonds in payment. These parties went to the trouble of preparing models with plans and specifications; all of which were afterwards duly submitted to the incompetent Secretary of the Confederate States Navy; but it resulted in nothing.

A considerable amount of the Government funds was lavished abroad upon the building of vessels which could by no possibility be got to sea under the Confederate flag while the war lasted; and to make matters worse, the Secretary had sent to England, as special agent for building or buying vessels, a man well known throughout the kingdom to be bankrupt in fame and fortune, who was hawking our government securities about the country at a ruinous rate of discount; and who inflicted much loss and injury upon the Confederate Government in various ways during his connection with it. The management of naval affairs abroad should have been left in the hands of Captain Bullock, the efficient agent of the Navy Department in England, who showed admirable tact in the conduct of affairs entrusted to him.

We stopped at the Burlington Hotel during our stay in London. There was none of the glare and glitter of an American hotel about this highly respectable establishment, no crowded *table d'hote* where the guests scrambled for food, and the waiters must be bribed to wait upon them; no gorgeous bar-room where the clinking of glasses resounds day and night, and no hotel clerk, with hair parted in the middle, who deems it a condescension to be civil. Everything was staid, quiet, orderly, and it must be added, rather slow and expensive.

As an illustration of the isolation of the boarders in an English hotel, it may be mentioned that two Southern ladies, acquaintances of a member of our party, were staying at the Burlington at the same time with ourselves, without our knowledge of the fact. Meals were usually served in the coffee room, the regular dinner consisting of a "joint," and one or two dishes of vegetables, any dish not included in this very plain bill of fare being furnished at an extra charge. Including fees to servants, etc., which are regularly entered in the bill, one may live very comfortably in an English hotel for five dollars a day, but not for less.

In thirty days from our arrival in England, the *Giraffe* was reported laden and ready for sea. Besides the purchases made through my agency, a large quantity of lithographic material had been bought by Major Ficklin for the Treasury Department; and twenty-six lithographers were engaged for the Confederate Government.

We took the train for Glasgow as soon as we were notified that the *Giraffe* was ready for sea; parting from our London friends with mutual good wishes and regrets.

There is a striking contrast between the scenery in the south of England, and that in the northern portion. As we approached the "iron country" even the fresh green woods disappeared, and for many miles on our way we could see tall chimneys pouring forth huge volumes of smoke, and we passed numerous coal pits, while the whole busy population seemed to be begrimed with coal dust and iron filings.

As we approached Glasgow the scenery again changed to broad and well cultivated plains in the immediate vicinity of the city. Its trade with Virginia and the West Indies laid the foundation of its present prosperity. To this day there are many descendants in Richmond of the old Scotch merchants who formerly traded in tobacco between that port and Glasgow, but of late years it has become chiefly noted for its iron ships and steamers, which are unsurpassed; and it is now, I believe, the second city in the United Kingdom in point of wealth and population. The Clyde, naturally an insignificant stream, has been deepened by art until it is now navigable for the largest vessels.

We were so busily occupied, during our brief stay, as to be able to see very little of the city or its environs. The city itself was enveloped in a fog during the whole time; its normal atmospheric condition, I presume; for once when we made a visit to the romantic "Brigg of Allan," we passed beyond the suburbs into a clear bright atmosphere; and on our return in the afternoon, we found the pall hanging over the city as usual.

We would have been delighted to take the advice of our hostess to see more of the land immortalized by Scott and Burns. "Ech, Sirs," she said, "but ye suld gae doon to the Heelands to see Scotland"; from which remark it may be reasonably inferred that she was a "Heeland" woman. We were painfully struck by the number of paupers and intoxicated females in the streets; and some of our party saw, for the first time in their lives, white women shoeless, and shivering in scanty rags, which scarcely concealed their nakedness, with the thermometer at the freezing point. Whitaker's British Almanac publishes, statistically, the *drinking* propensities of the population of the three kingdoms, from which it appears that there were consumed per head in 1869—

Malt 1,989 bushels in England; spirits 591 gallons. Malt 509 bushels in Ireland; spirits 873 gallons. Malt 669 bushels in Scotland; spirits 1,576 gallons.

The inventory taken on board the *Giraffe*, after she was turned over to the Confederate Government, showed over *two hundred* pitchers and ladles for hot punch! We came to the conclusion that Scotch babies were weaned upon this beverage, for the law forbade the carrying of that number of grown passengers by the *Giraffe*.

Having secured the services of a sailing captain, British laws not allowing the clearance of a vessel under the British flag, except under the command of one who holds a certificate of competence, we sent our luggage on board one evening, and sat down to our last meal on British soil. There were many guests at the table; several of our friends having come on from London to see us take our departure, and toasts were duly and enthusiastically drank to the success of "the cause." The privileged old head-waiter, dressed in professional black, (and ridiculously like an old magpie as he hopped about the room with his head on one side,) "whose custom it was of an afternoon" to get drunk, but always with Scotch decorum, nodded approval of the festivities, until, overcome by his feelings (or Usquebaugh) he was obliged to withdraw.

We bade adieu to our friends late at night, and went on board early next morning. In addition to the Scotch artisans already mentioned, there were several young gentlemen who were about to return home in the *Giraffe*. These youths had been prosecuting their studies in Germany. They were now about to return home to enter the army. Two of them, Messrs. Price and Blair, are now Professors in Virginia Colleges, after doing their duty as brave and faithful soldiers during the war. It is well known that many thousands of young men, the flower of the South, served as privates during the whole of our struggle for independence; and it is equally well known that they never flinched from dangers or privations.

Many years ago an expedition under the command of Lieutenant Strain, of the United States Navy, was sent to make a reconnaissance across the Isthmus of Darien. The party lost their way among the morasses and almost impenetrable forests, and endured frightful hardships. But the officers survived, while many of the men succumbed to fatigue and famine. During our war, the youths of gentle blood and tender nurture displayed equally wonderful endurance.

We parted from the Major on the wharf before going on board. He promised to meet us in Richmond; preferring himself to return via. New York; and we did not doubt his ability to keep his promise; for he seemed to experience no difficulty in passing and re-passing through the lines at his pleasure during the war. He was in Washington, indeed, at the time when President Lincoln was assassinated, and was arrested as an accomplice in that great crime. His numerous friends who had so often suffered from his practical jokes, would have been pleased no doubt, to see how he appreciated the jest, when his head was tied up in a feather pillow to prevent him from defrauding the law by committing suicide in the murderer's cell. The shrill sound of a whistle was heard in the theatre just before Booth committed the act; and when the Major was arrested in his bed at the hotel a few hours afterwards, a whistle was found in his pocket. It was damaging evidence, but he escaped prosecution as an accomplice by adopting the advice once given by Mr. Toney Weller, and proving an alibi.

CHAPTER 7

Blockade Running

Our voyage to Madeira was uneventful with the exception of a heavy gale of wind, during which the *Giraffe* showed her superb qualities as a sea boat.

We were hospitably entertained during our three days' stay at Funchal. The process of coaling ship there is a tedious one, the port being an open roadstead, and there are no wharves. With a moderate breeze blowing on or along shore, all communication is interrupted. Loading and unloading ships is accomplished by lighters; and passengers are carried to and fro in surf boats which are expertly managed by their crews. The vines had failed for several years previous to our visit; but the inhabitants had substituted the cultivation of vegetables for which they found a market on the continent and in England; and the numerous cultivated patches along the mountain sides presented a very pretty appearance from the anchorage—laid out as they were with seemingly geometrical precision.

The hardy little horses could be hired very cheaply, and the justly extolled natural beauties of the island in the vicinity of Funchal were fully explored. The greater portion of it is quite inaccessible except on foot, but the tough little native ponies which are as sure footed as goats perform wonderful feats in the way of climbing, and are quite equal to the double duty of carrying their riders, and dragging along their owner who holds by one hand to the pony's tail while he occasionally prods him with a sharp stick held in the other hand.

This island is, as every one knows, of volcanic origin; although its volcanoes are now either dormant or extinct; and its lofty vertical cliffs rise abruptly from the ocean. The highest peak in the island is more than six thousand feet above the level of the sea. The disintegrated lava forms the best soil in the world for the grape; and the south side of the island, from its more favourable exposure to the sun, is supposed to produce the more delicately flavoured wine. Wonderful stories are told of the exquisite sense of taste possessed by the professional "tasters" who never swallow the wine. So soon as they indulge in this luxury they lose the faculty of nice discrimination.

We slept securely under the "Stars and Stripes," our hotel being kept by a "Yankee" who hoisted the flag upon his house-top every day, and was not so cosmopolitan, perhaps I should say not so politic, as our St. Thomas friend. He soothed his conscience for associating with "rebels," and avenged himself by charging us heavily, and, no doubt, congratulated himself after our departure, upon having "spoiled the Egyptians."

We received many courtesies from Mr. B., an English gentleman, and his family. Our susceptible young men lost their hearts with his *seven* beautiful daughters, all of them fair, tall, and stately.

As soon as the *Giraffe* was coaled we took our departure for St. John's, Porto Rico. A sea-voyage has elsewhere been described in two lines:

Sometimes we ship a sea,
Sometimes we see a ship.

The monotony of our voyage was rarely disturbed by either of these incidents.

After two days' detention at St. John's for the purpose of coaling we got under way for that haven of blockade-runners, El Dorado of adventurers, and paradise of wreckers and darkies—filthy Nassau. In making our way to this port we had a foretaste of some of the risks and dangers to be subsequently encountered.

In order to economize coal and to lessen the risk of capture I determined to approach Nassau by the "Tongue of Ocean," a deep indentation in the sea bounded on the south by the Bahama Banks; and to reach the "Tongue" it was necessary to cross the whole extent of the "Banks" from Elbow Key lighthouse. On arriving off the light-house we were disappointed in our hope of finding a pilot, and no alternative was left but to attempt the transit without one, as we had not a sufficient supply of coal to enable us to pursue any other course. Our charts showed twelve feet of water all over that portion of the Banks and the *Giraffe* was drawing eleven feet; but the innumerable black dots on the chart showed where the dangerous coral heads were nearly "awash." On the other hand, we knew there could be no "swell" in such an expanse of shallow water; so waving adieu to the keeper of the light-house we pointed the *Giraffe's* bow for the Banks, which showed ahead of us smooth as a lake, and almost milk white.

It was early in the morning when we started, and the distance to be run to the "Tongue" was only sixty or seventy miles. Taking my station in the fore-rigging I could easily direct the helmsman bow to avoid those treacherous black spots. It was the Florida Reef over again, and my experience in surveying that coast stood us in good stead here. We were so fortunate, indeed, as never once to touch the bottom although the lead frequently showed less than twelve feet; and about 3 o'clock in the afternoon the welcome blue water showed itself ahead. It would have been impossible to make the transit in cloudy weather; but the day was fortunately clear. Occasionally when a "trade" cloud would approach the sun, we would slow down or stop until it had passed by, when the black patches would again be visible. The iron plates of the *Giraffe* would have been pierced as completely as if made of pasteboard, if she had come into contact even at low speed with those jagged coral heads. Before dark we were out of danger, and next morning came to anchor in the harbour of Nassau.

Nassau was a busy place during the war; the chief depot of supplies for the Confederacy, and the port to which most of the cotton was shipped. Its proximity to the ports of Charleston and Wilmington gave it superior advantages, while it was easily accessible to the swift, light draft blockade-runners; all of which carried Bahama bank pilots who knew every channel, while the United States cruisers having no Bank pilots and drawing more water were compelled to keep the open sea. Occasionally one of the latter would heave to outside the harbour and send in a boat to communicate with the American Consul; but their usual cruising ground was off Abaco Light.

Nassau is situated upon the island of New Providence, one of the Bahamas, and is the chief town and capital of the group. All of the islands are surrounded by coral reefs and shoals, through which are channels more or less intricate. That wonderful "River in the Sea"—the Gulf Stream—which flows between the Florida coast and the Bahama Banks is only forty miles broad between the nearest opposite points; but there is no harbour on that part of the Florida coast.

The distance from Charleston to Nassau is about five hundred miles, and from Wilmington about five hundred and fifty. Practically, however, they were equi-distant because blockade-runners bound from either port, in order to evade the cruisers lying in wait off Abaco, were compelled to give that headland a wide berth, by keeping well to the eastward of it. But in avoiding Scylla they ran the risk of striking upon Charybdis; for the dangerous reefs of Eleuthera were fatal to many vessels.

The chief industries of the islands before the war were the collection and exportation of sponges, corals, etc., and wrecking, to which was added, during the war, the lucrative trade of picking and stealing. The inhabitants may be classed as "amphibious," and are known among sailors by the generic name of "Conchs." The wharves of Nassau, during the war, were always piled high with cotton, and huge warehouses were stored full of supplies for the Confederacy. The harbour was crowded at times, with lead-coloured, short masted, rakish looking steamers; the streets alive with bustle and activity during day time and swarming with drunken revellers by night.

Every nationality on earth, nearly, was represented there; the high wages ashore and afloat, tempting adventurers of the baser sort; and the prospect of enormous profits offering equally strong inducements to capitalists of a speculative turn. The monthly wages of a sailor on board a blockade-runner was one hundred dollars in gold, and fifty dollars bounty at the end of a successful trip; and this could be accomplished under favourable circumstances in seven days. The captains and pilots sometimes received as much as five thousand dollars besides perquisites.

All of the cotton shipped on account of the Confederate Government was landed and transferred to a mercantile firm in Nassau, who received a commission for assuming ownership. It was then shipped under the British or other neutral flag to Europe. The firm is reputed to have made many thousands of dollars by these commissions. But, besides the cotton shipped by the Confederate Government, many private companies and individuals were engaged in the trade; and it was computed (so large were the gains) that the owner could afford to lose a vessel and cargo after two successful voyages.

Three or four steamers were wholly owned by the Confederate Government; a few more were owned by it in part, and the balance were private property; but these last were compelled to carry out, as portion of their cargo, cotton on government account, and to bring in supplies. On board the government steamers, the crew which was shipped abroad, and under the articles regulating the "merchant marine," received the same wages as were paid on board the other blockade-runners; but the captains and subordinate officers of the government steamers who belonged to the Confederate States Navy, and the pilots, who were detailed from the army for this service, received the pay in gold of their respective grades.

As the *Giraffe's* crew was shipped only for the voyage to Nassau "and a market," it was necessary to cancel the engagement of those who did not wish to follow her fortunes further. A few of them preferring their discharge were paid off, and provided with a passage to England; and the balance signed articles for Havana "and a market."

Everything being in readiness, we sailed on December 26th, 1862. Having on board a Charleston pilot, as well as one for Wilmington, I had not determined, on sailing, which port to attempt; but having made the land near Charleston bar during thick weather on the night of the 28th, our pilot was afraid to venture further. We made an offing, therefore, before daylight; and circumstances favouring Wilmington, we approached the western bar on the night of December 29th. We had been biding our time since twelve o'clock that day close in to the shore about forty miles southwest of the bar and in the deep bay formed by the coast between Wilmington and Charleston.

The weather had been so clear and the sea so smooth that we had communicated with the Confederate pickets at several points along the coast; and no sail was visible even from aloft until about three o'clock in the afternoon, when a cruiser hove in sight to the north and east. As she was coasting along the land and approaching us we turned the *Giraffe's* bow away from her, and got up more steam, easily preserving our distance, as the stranger was steaming at a low rate of speed. A little while before sunset the strange steamer wore round, and we immediately followed her example, gradually lessening the distance between us, and an hour or more after dark we had the pleasure of passing inside of her at anchor off New River Inlet. She was evidently blockading that harbour, and had run down the coast to reconnoitre.

Before approaching the bar I had adopted certain precautions against disaster which I ever afterwards followed. Any one who showed an open light when we were near the fleet was liable to the penalty of death upon the spot; a cool, steady leadsman was stationed on each quarter to give the soundings; a staunch old quartermaster took the wheel and a kedge, bent to a stout hawser, was slung at each quarter. All lights were extinguished; the fire-room hatch covered over with a tarpaulin; and a hood fitted over the binnacle, with a small circular opening for the helmsman to see the compass through the aperture.

About ten o'clock we passed inside the first ship of the blockading fleet, about five miles outside the bar; and four or five others appeared in quick succession as the *Giraffe* was cutting rapidly through the smooth water. We were going at full speed when, with a shock that threw nearly every one on board off his feet, the steamer was brought up "all standing" and hard and fast aground! The nearest blockader was fearfully close to us, and all seemed lost. We had struck upon "the Lump," a small sandy knoll two or three miles outside the bar with deep water on both sides of it. That knoll was the "rock ahead" during the whole war, of the blockade-runners, for it was impossible in the obscurity of night to judge accurately of the distance to the coast, and there were no landmarks or bearings which would enable them to steer clear of it. Many a ton of valuable freight has been launched overboard there; and, indeed, all the approaches to Wilmington are paved as thickly with valuables as a certain place is said to be with good intentions.

The first order was to lower the two quarter boats: in one of them were packed the Scotch lithographers who were safely landed; and a kedge was lowered into the other with orders to the officer in charge to pull off shore and drop the kedge. The risk, though imminent, was much reduced after our panic stricken passengers had got fairly away from the ship; and the spirits of officers and crew rose to meet the emergency. The glimmer of a light, or an incautiously loud order would bring a broadside from that frowning battery crashing through our bulwarks. So near the goal (I thought) and now to fail! but I did not despair. To execute the order to drop the kedge, it was necessary to directly approach one of the blockaders, and so near to her did they let it go, that the officer of the boat was afraid to call out that it had been dropped; and muffled the oars as he returned to make his report. Fortunately, the tide was rising.

After twenty or thirty minutes of trying suspense, the order was given "to set taut on the hawser," and our pulses beat high as the stern of the *Giraffe* slowly and steadily turned seaward. In fact, she swung round upon her stem as upon a pivot. As soon as the hawser "trended" right astern, the engineer was ordered to "back hard," and in a very few revolutions of the wheels the ship slid rapidly off into deep water. The hawser was instantly cut, and we headed directly for the bar channel. We were soon out of danger from the blockading fleet; but as we drew in toward Fort Caswell, one of the look-outs on the wheel-house (who, like the thief in Shakespeare, "feared each bush an officer") would every now and then say to the pilot, "that looks like a boat on the star-board bow, Mr. D."

"There are breakers on the port-bow, Mr. D." And at last "There is a rock right ahead, Mr. D."

At which last remark, D., losing all patience, exclaimed, "G——d A——y, man, there isn't a rock as big as my hat in the whole d——d state of North Carolina." A too sweeping assertion, but quite true as applied to the coast. We passed safely over the bar; and steaming up the river, anchored off Smithville a little before midnight of the 29th of December, 1862.

The Scotch lithographers found abundant employment in Richmond, as the Government "paper mills" were running busily during the whole war; but the style of their work was not altogether faultless, for it was said that the counterfeit notes, made at the North, and extensively circulated through the South, could be easily detected by the superior execution of the engraving upon them!

The natural advantages of Wilmington for blockade-running were very great, chiefly owing to the fact, that there are two separate and distinct approaches to Cape Fear River, *i.e.*, either by "New Inlet" to the north of Smith's Island, or by the "western bar" to the south of it. This island is ten or eleven miles in length; but the Frying Pan Shoals extend ten or twelve miles further south, making the distance by sea between the two bars thirty miles or more, although the direct distance between them is only six or seven miles. From Smithville, a little village nearly equi-distant from either bar, both blockading fleets could be distinctly seen, and the outward bound blockade-runners could take their choice through which of them to run the gauntlet.

The inward bound blockade-runners, too, were guided by circumstances of wind and weather; selecting that bar over which they would cross, after they had passed the Gulf Stream; and shaping their course accordingly. The approaches to both bars were clear of danger, with the single exception of the "Lump" before mentioned; and so regular are the soundings that the shore can be coasted for miles within a stone's throw of the breakers.

These facts explain why the United States fleet were unable wholly to stop blockade-running. It was, indeed, impossible to do so; the result to the very close of the war proves this assertion; for in spite of the vigilance of the fleet, many blockade-runners were afloat when Fort Fisher was captured. In truth the passage through the fleet was little dreaded; for although the blockade-runner might receive a shot or two, she was rarely disabled; and in proportion to the increase of the fleet, the greater would be the danger (we knew,) of their firing into each other. As the boys before the deluge used to say, they would be very apt "to miss the cow and kill the calf."

The chief danger was upon the open sea; many of the light cruisers having great speed. As soon as one of them discovered a blockade-runner during daylight she would attract other cruisers in the vicinity by sending up a dense column of smoke, visible for many miles in clear weather. A "cordon" of fast steamers stationed ten or fifteen miles apart *inside the Gulf Stream*, and in the course from Nassau and Bermuda to

Wilmington and Charleston, would have been more effectual in stopping blockade-running than the whole United States Navy concentrated off those ports; and it was unaccountable to us why such a plan did not occur to good Mr. Welles; but it was not our place to suggest it. I have no doubt, however, that the fraternity to which I then belonged would have unanimously voted thanks and a service of plate to the Hon. Secretary of the United States Navy for this oversight.

I say *inside the Gulf Stream*, because every experienced captain of a blockade-runner made a point to cross "the stream" early enough in the afternoon, if possible, to establish the ship's position by chronometer so as to escape the influence of that current upon his dead reckoning. The lead always gave indication of our distance from the land, but not, of course, of our position; and the numerous salt works along the coast, where evaporation was produced by fire, and which were at work night and day were visible long before the low coast could be seen.

Occasionally the whole inward voyage would be made under adverse conditions. Cloudy, thick weather and heavy gales would prevail so as to prevent any solar or lunar observations, and reduce the dead reckoning to mere guess work. In these cases the nautical knowledge and judgment of the captain would be taxed to the utmost. The current of the Gulf Stream varies in velocity and (within certain limits) in direction; and the stream, itself almost as well defined as a river within its banks under ordinary circumstances, is impelled by a strong gale toward the direction in which the wind is blowing, overflowing its banks as it were. The counter current, too, inside of the Gulf Stream is much influenced by the prevailing winds.

Upon one occasion, while in command of the *R. E. Lee*, we had experienced very heavy and thick weather; and had crossed the Stream and struck soundings about midday. The weather then clearing so that we could obtain an altitude near meridian we found ourselves at least forty miles north of our supposed position and near the shoals which extend in a southerly direction off Cape Lookout. It would be more perilous to run out to sea than to continue on our course, for we had passed through the off shore line of blockaders, and the sky had become perfectly clear. I determined to personate a transport bound to Beaufort, which was in the possession of the United States forces, and the coaling station of the fleet blockading Wilmington. The risk of detection was not very great, for many of the captured blockade-runners were used as transports and dispatch vessels.

Shaping our course for Beaufort, and slowing down, as we were in no haste to get there, we passed several vessels, showing United States colours to them all.

Just as we were crossing through the ripple of shallow water off the "tail" of the shoals, we dipped our colours to a sloop of war which passed three or four miles to the south of us. The courtesy was promptly responded to; but I have no doubt her captain thought me a lubberly and careless seaman to shave the shoals so closely. We stopped the engines when no vessel was in sight; and I was relieved from a heavy burden of anxiety as the sun sank below the horizon; and the course was shaped at full speed for Masonboro' Inlet.

A few days after our arrival at Wilmington the *Giraffe* was transferred to the Confederate Government, and named the *R. E. Lee*; and thenceforward carried the Confederate flag.

Our friend the Major fulfilled his promise of meeting me in Richmond, having made his way across the Potomac. He made a gallant effort to get possession of the ship; but Mr. Seddon, who had succeeded Mr. Randolph as Secretary of War during our absence, contended that the Government had a juster claim; and the facts of the case were too stubborn even for the Major's determined persistence.

The Secretary of War having carried his point, the Major directed his efforts towards another quarter, and more successfully. Indeed he rarely failed in any enterprise requiring nerve, perseverance, tact, and ability; and it may well be added that he seemed to accumulate wealth to enjoy the pleasure of spending it worthily. His unostentatious charities during the war were almost boundless; and hundreds of widows and orphans blessed him for the relief which he extended to them in those dark days, when even medicines were contraband of war, and the simplest necessaries of life were beyond the reach of nearly every one in the Confederacy.

CHAPTER 8

The West Indies

Before sailing with our cargo of cotton for Nassau, a signal officer was detailed for the ship, (signal stations having been established along the coast for the benefit of the blockade-runners;) and I was compelled to discharge my pilot Dyer. He and the sailing captain, who was to take passage with us, his engagement having terminated with the transfer of the vessel to the Confederate flag, had been quarrelling incessantly during my absence from Wilmington, and had finally become mortal foes. An hour or more after my return to the ship, while sitting in the cabin, I heard loud and angry altercation overhead; and going on deck, I saw Dyer pacing up and down the wharf, along side which the *Lee* was lying; while the sailing captain was bidding him defiance from the steamer's deck; Dyer with a drawn knife in his hand, and the captain armed with a handspike. They had exhausted their vocabulary of abuse, but neither was disposed to invade the enemy's territory.

At last Dyer cried out "Come ashore you d——d English hog, and I'll make mince meat of you!"

I shall never forget the expression of the captain's face at this cruel taunt. He was literally struck speechless for a moment; then turning to me and drawing himself up with a thumb in his arm-hole, and the handspike over his shoulder, he exclaimed, "Now, sir, isn't that *too* bad! Do I *look* like a Henglish og?"

To this pathetic appeal, I could but answer "no," but the fact was they bore a ludicrous resemblance to two boars about to engage in mortal combat; the captain, with his jolly, rosy face and portly figure, not at all unlike a sleek, well fed "White Chester," and Dyer quite as much resembling a lean, lank, wiry "razorback" native of his own pine woods.

I discharged Dyer. The poor fellow's subsequent fate was a sad one. While acting as pilot of a blockade-runner, inward bound, he committed the folly one day of saying that he would put a steamer under his charge ashore, before he would be captured. The remark was overheard and treasured up by some of the crew; and a night or two afterwards the steamer ran aground on the bar in the attempt to enter Cape Fear River, and was deserted. As she was under the shelter of the guns of Fort Caswell, a boat from shore was sent off to her next morning, and poor Dyer was found in a dying condition on the deck with his skull fractured. He had paid for his folly with his life.

Our first voyage to Nassau was made without any unusual incident. The Major took passage with us by permission of the Secretary of War, and his practical jokes amused every one except the butt of them; even the aggrieved party, himself, being frequently obliged to laugh at his own expense.

There were two very young lieutenants of the Confederate Navy then in Nassau, on their way to Europe; the senior of whom *ranking* the other by one or two days, assumed much authority over him. One day the Major with the help of an accomplice, who was supposed to be able to imitate my handwriting, addressed an official letter to the senior in my name, informing him that both of them had been reported to me for un-officerlike and unbecoming conduct, and requiring them to repair immediately on board the *Lee* with their luggage, as I felt it to be an imperative duty to take them back to the Confederacy for trial by court-martial.

The junior demurred, believing it to be a hoax, but the senior peremptorily ordered him to accompany him on board.

They were caught in a drenching shower on their way to the *Lee*; and they made their appearance in the cabin in a sorry plight, reporting themselves "in obedience to orders," handing me the written document. As I pronounced it a forgery, the junior turned to the senior and exclaimed: "What did I tell you? didn't I say it was a hoax of that d——d Major Ficklen?"

They started to the shore, vowing vengeance; but the Major had posted his sentinels at every street corner near the landing, and successfully eluded them. They were to sail that afternoon at four o'clock; and after a fruitless chase, went to the hotel to get dinner. While sitting at the table, and some time after soup was served, a waiter came to them "with Major Ficklen's compliments and the pleasure of a glass of champagne with them." After a hurried consultation, they decided to bury the hatchet; and bowed over their wine to the Major, who had just slipped into a seat reserved for him at the other end of the long and crowded table, and was smiling graciously in their direction. As Ficklen bade them "good-bye," he said "Don't forget me, my sons!"

"No, indeed," they replied, "you may swear we never will!"

Seeing the necessity, while at Nassau, of carrying a Bahama Banks pilot, I engaged our worthy old skipper, Captain Dick Watkins, who served under my command for many months, maintaining and deserving the respect of all on board. His son, and only heir to his name and fortune, Napoleon Bonaparte, gave him much anxiety. "Ah, Sir," he said on one occasion, "dat b——y's heddication has cost me a sight of money, as much as ten dollars a year for two or three years, and he don't know nothing hardly."

During one of our voyages he had left his wife quite sick at home. My young friend Johnny T——was endeavouring to console him. "But the ole 'oman is *mighty* sick, Master Johnny," said the old fellow, "and I don't spect to see her no more." Johnny's heart was touched. The silence was broken by Captain Dick after a long pause, "dere are some mighty pretty yaller gals in *Nassau*, Master Johnny!"

He had the profoundest respect for the head of the firm of A——y and Co. in Nassau, the "King Conch" as he was irreverently styled by us outside barbarians. Speaking of the firm upon one occasion he assured me the members were as wealthy as the "*Roths children.*" My good purser and the old captain were fast friends, the former fighting the old fellow's battles in Rebeldom; and once, when the latter was unjustly treated in Wilmington, the purser "took the daggers," and bore him triumphantly through the difficulty.

We made two or three trips between Wilmington and Nassau during the winter of 1862-3 encountering no extraordinary hazards. During one of them we arrived within ten or twelve miles of the western bar too early in the night to cross it, as the ebb tide was still running; and it was always my custom to cross the bar on a rising tide, if possible. All the usual preparations had been made on board for running through the fleet, and as no sail was in sight we steamed cautiously in toward the land until we arrived within a cable's length of the shore, and in the dense shadow of a comparatively high bluff. Here we dropped a kedge and rode by the hawser.

Although there was no moon, the stars were shining brightly; and the air was so calm and still, that the silence was oppressive. While we were lying in the friendly shadow of the bluff, one of the blockading fleet could be occasionally seen from our deck, steaming slowly along upon her "beat" a short distance outside of us. When the time arrived for making the dash at the bar, the kedge was run up to the bows by willing hands, and the *Lee* started at full speed. When the land was once fairly got hold of, and our exact position known, the chances were ten to one in our favour. No blockader could get inshore of us to cut us off from the bar, and we believed that we could either go by or go over anything in our course; and in extremity we could beach the vessel with the probability of being able to save most, if not the whole of the cargo.

During the month of March, 1863, the *Lee's* port of destination was St. George's, Bermuda. This island is easily accessible on the southern side, and was much resorted to by blockade-runners. Surrounded on all other sides by dangerous coral reefs, which extend for many miles into deep water, a vessel of heavy draft can approach from the south within a cable's length of the shore. A light of the first class at the west end of the group composing the "Bermudas," is visible for many miles in clear weather. It may as well be mentioned here, that the blockade-runners rarely approached *any* head land during daylight; "preferring darkness rather than light."

The agent of the Confederate Government, Major Walker, with his staff of assistants, lived at St. George's; and he and his accomplished wife always welcomed their compatriots with genuine hospitality. The house of Mr. Black (an assistant of the Major) was also open to us, and no sick exile from home will ever forget the tender nursing of Mrs. Black and the kindness of that whole family. The little graveyard attached to the Episcopal church at St. George's, contains all that is mortal of several gallant youths from the south, who died of yellow fever; but they were soothed in the hours of their last illness by Christian counsel, and by tender hands.

The white natives of the island, too, extended many attentions and civilities to Confederates, so that St. George's became not only a harbour of refuge, but a pleasant resting place after the excitement and fatigue of an outward voyage.

The same antagonism which prevails between the white and the black races, wherever they live together upon equal terms, exists in Bermuda. People are classed there as "*coloured* and *plain*" and a fine of one pound sterling is imposed for calling the former "negroes." There must be a natural antipathy between the two races; or at least it seems to exist in the heart of the negro, for wherever he has the power, he shows his dislike and jealousy of the white man. In Haiti, since the French inhabitants were murdered, the jealousy and hatred of the negroes have been directed against the mulattoes, who have been nearly exterminated; and the whites in Jamaica would have shared the same fate at the hands of a brutal horde of black savages a few years ago, but for the premature exposure of the plot, and the vigorous action of the Governor of the island.

In the model republic of Liberia no white man can obtain the right of citizenship, own real estate, nor sit upon a jury. Nowhere in the world did there exist the same kindly relation between the two races, as in the South before the war; and even now, the older negroes seek aid and advice, when in difficulties, from their former owners, although they have been misled by unprincipled adventurers, by whom they have been taught to distrust them in politics. A short time ago Dr. B———, a Virginia gentleman, was asked by a Northerner his opinion of the negroes' feelings toward the Southern people. "I will tell you," replied Dr. B. "If you and I were candidates for the same office, you would get every negro's vote; but, if one of them wanted advice or assistance he would come to me or some other southerner."

The group composing the "Bermudas" still justifies the reputation given to it by one of the British admirals of the "olden time." The "Bermoothees," he records in his quaintly written journal, "is a hellish place for thunder, lightning, and storms." Shakespeare, too, sends Ariel to "fetch dew" from the "still vexed Bermoothes" for his exacting master Prospero. But although gales of wind during the winter, and thunder storms in the summer, are so prevalent, the climate is delightful. There are upward of three hundred islands in the group, most of them mere barren coral rocks; and the largest, St. George's, is not more than three miles long, and about a mile in width. The roads are cut out of the soft coral, which hardens by exposure to the atmosphere, and are perfect.

There are several very curious natural caves about five miles distant from St. George's; and near one of them is still pointed out the calabash tree under which the Irish poet, Tom Moore, is said to have composed one of his sonnets to *Nea*, who afterwards became the wife of Mr. Tucker, and left many descendants on the island. The venerable old gentleman was living, in his ninetieth year, when I was last in St. George's; and although the bride of his youth, and his rival the poet, had been long mouldering in their graves, he was still so jealous of the latter that he would not allow his great-grandchildren to keep a copy of the poet's works in the house.

The only indigenous tree upon the islands, I believe, is the cedar; the oleander, which now grows everywhere, having been introduced by Mr. Tucker. Nearly all of the tropical fruits grow there, and many indigenous to the temperate zone; but the staple products are potatoes and onions, chiefly for the New York market, and arrow root. The waters teem with fish of the most brilliantly beautiful colours. An ingenious individual has succeeded in taming a number, by availing himself of a natural cavity in the coral situated close to the shore and a few miles distant from St. George's. The sea water, percolating through the coral, supplies the basin. At a whistle the tame fish swim close to the edge and feed from one's hand.

There is a naval station at "Ireland Island," and a floating dock (which was built in England and towed out,) capable of taking in the largest-sized man of war. The naval officers attached to the dock-yard, and to the men of war, were always friendly and more than civil to Confederates; being sometimes, indeed, too profuse in their hospitality. Upon one occasion, Col.——a personal friend of mine, had obtained a furlough, and permission to make a trip in the *Lee*, for the sake of his health, broken by the hardships of a campaign in northern Virginia. The purser, who was always ready for a "lark," and the Colonel, who was of an inquiring turn of mind, paid a visit to the dock-yard. After an inspection of it, they went on board several of the men of war in harbour, receiving on board each of them refreshments, solid and liquid.

They had crossed over to Ireland Island in a sail-boat, and when about to return, were escorted to the wharf by a party of officers. Their boat was lying outside of another, containing a fat old washerwoman; and Col.——, who had had no experience in boating in his life, except "paddling his own canoe" upon a mill pond in Amelia county, Va., stopped to exchange farewell salutations with the party of officers on the wharf, while he stood with one foot in the "stern sheets" of the washerwoman's boat, and the other in his own. The boatman forward, ignorant of the critical state of affairs, hoisted the jib, and the boat, under the influence of a stiff breeze, began to "pay off" before the wind. Before Col.——could "realize the situation," he was in the attitude of the Colossus of Rhodes. The purser promptly seized one of his legs, and the fat washerwoman with equal presence of mind, laid hold of the other. Each was determined not to let go, and the strain upon the Colonel must have been terrific; but he was equal to the emergency.

Taking in the whole situation, he deliberately drew his watch out of his pocket, and holding it high above his head with both hands, he said, with his usually imperturbable calmness, "Well I reckon you had better let go!" His endeavours to protect his watch proved to have been fruitless; the purser indeed always insists that he touched bottom in three fathoms of water. He returned on board the *Lee* to be wrung out and dried.

CHAPTER 9

Passing Through the Fleet

After discharging our cargo of cotton and loading with supplies for the Confederate Government, chiefly for the army of Northern Virginia, we sailed for Wilmington in the latter part of the month of March. Our return voyage was uneventful, until we reached the coast near Masonborough Inlet, distant about nine miles north of the "New Inlet" bar.

The weather had been pleasant during the voyage, and we had sighted the *fires* from the salt works along the coast, but before we could get hold of the land, a little before midnight, a densely black cloud made its appearance to the north and east; and the rapidity with which it rose and enlarged, indicated too surely that a heavy gale was coming from that quarter. We had been unable to distinguish any landmark before the storm burst in all its fury upon us, and the rain poured in torrents. Our supply of coals was too limited to enable us, with prudence, to put to sea again; and of course, the marks or ranges for crossing the bar would not be visible fifty yards in such thick weather.

Being quite confident of our position, however, I determined to run down the coast, and anchor off the bar till daylight. Knowing the "trend" of the land north of New Inlet bar, the engine was slowed down and the lead kept going on both sides. The sounding continued quite regular three and three and a quarter fathoms, with the surf thundering within a stone's throw on our starboard beam, and nothing visible in the blinding torrents of rain. I knew that if my calculated position was correct, the water would shoal very suddenly just before reaching the bar; but a trying hour or more of suspense had passed before the welcome fact was announced by the leadsmen.

The course and distance run, and the soundings up to this point proved, beyond doubt, that we had now reached the "horse shoe" north of New Inlet bar. At the moment when both of the leadsmen almost simultaneously called out "and a quarter less three," the helm was put hard a-starboard, and the *Lee's* bow was pointed seaward. We could not prudently anchor in less than five fathoms water, as the sea was rising rapidly; and that depth would carry us into the midst of the blockading fleet at anchor outside. It seemed an age before the cry came from the leadsmen "by the mark five."

The *Lee* was instantly stopped, and one of the bower anchors let go, veering to thirty fathoms on the chain. The cable was then well stoppered at the "bitts," and unshackled; and two men stationed at the stopper, with axes, and the order to cut the lashings, instantly, when so ordered; the fore-staysail was loosed, and hands stationed at the halliards; and the chief engineer directed to keep up a full head of steam.

The night wore slowly away; and once or twice we caught a glimpse, by a flash of lightning, of the blockading fleet around us, rolling and pitching in the heavy sea. The watch having been set, the rest of the officers and crew were permitted to go below, except the chief engineer and the pilot. We paced the bridge, anxiously waiting for daylight. It came at last, and there, right astern of us, looming up through the mist and rain, was the "Mound." We had only to steer for it, to be on our right course for crossing the bar. The stoppers were cut, the engine started ahead, and the fore stay-sail hoisted. As the chain rattled through the hawse-hole, the *Lee* wore rapidly around, and the Confederate flag was run up to the peak as she dashed toward the bar with the speed of a greyhound slipped from the leash.

The bar was a sheet of foam and surf, breaking sheer across the channel; but the great length of the *Lee* enabled her to ride over three or four of the short chopping seas at once, and she never touched the bottom. In less than half an hour from the time when we slipped our chain under the guns of the fleet, we had passed beyond Fort Fisher, and were on our way up the river to Wilmington.

The "Mound" was an artificial one, erected by Colonel Lamb, who commanded Fort Fisher. Two heavy guns were mounted upon it, and it eventually became a site for a light, and very serviceable to blockade-runners; but even at this period, it was an excellent landmark. Joined by a long low isthmus of sand with the higher main land, its regular conical shape enabled the blockade-runners easily to identify it from the offing; and in clear weather, it showed plain and distinct against the sky at night. I believe the military men used to laugh slyly at the Colonel for undertaking its erection, predicting that it would not stand; but the result showed the contrary; and whatever difference of opinion may have existed with regard to its value as a military position, there can be but one as to its utility to the blockade-runners, for it was not a landmark, alone, along this monotonous coast; but one of the range lights for crossing New Inlet bar was placed on it. Seamen will appreciate at its full value, this advantage; but it may be stated, for the benefit of the unprofessional reader, that while the compass bearing of an object does not enable a pilot to steer a vessel with sufficient accuracy through a narrow channel, *range lights* answer the purpose completely. These lights were only set after signals had been exchanged between the blockade-runner and the shore station, and were removed immediately after the vessel had entered the river. The range lights were changed as circumstances required; for the New Inlet channel, itself, was and is constantly changing, being materially affected both in depth of water, and in its course, by a heavy gale of wind or a severe freshet in Cape Fear River.

The *Lee* continued to make her regular trips either to Nassau or Bermuda, as circumstances required, during the summer of 1863; carrying abroad cotton and naval stores, and bringing in "hardware," as munitions of war were then invoiced. Usually the time selected for sailing was during the "dark of the moon," but upon one occasion, a new pilot had been detailed for duty on board, who failed in many efforts to get the ship over the "rip," a shifting sand bar a mile or more inside the true bar. More than a week of valuable time had thus been lost, but the exigencies of the army being at that time more than usually urgent, I determined to run what appeared to be a very great risk.

The tide serving at ten o'clock, we succeeded in crossing the rip at that hour, and as we passed over New Inlet bar, the moon rose in a cloudless sky. It was a calm night too, and the regular beat of our paddles through the smooth water sounded to our ears ominously loud. As we closely skirted the shore, the blockading vessels were plainly visible to us, some at anchor, some under way; and some of them so near to us that we saw, or fancied we saw, with our night glasses, the men on watch on their forecastles; but as we were inside of them all, and invisible against the background of the land, we passed beyond them undiscovered. The roar of the surf breaking upon the beach, prevented the noise of our paddles from being heard.

The *Lee*'s head was not pointed seaward, however, until we had run ten or twelve miles along the land so close to the breakers that we could almost have tossed a biscuit into them, and no vessel was to be seen in any direction. Discovery of us by the fleet would probably have been fatal to us, but the risk was really not so great as it appeared; for, as I had been informed by a blockade-runner who had been once captured and released, being a British subject, the vigilance on board the blockading fleet was much relaxed during the moon-lit nights. The vessels were sent to Beaufort to coal at these times. My informant was an officer of the British Navy, and was the guest, for a few days after his capture, of Captain Patterson then commanding the blockading fleet off the Cape Fear. Speaking of the arduous service, P. remarked to him, that he never undressed nor retired to bed, during the dark nights; but could enjoy those luxuries when the moon was shining. On this hint I acted.

It was about this time that I adopted an expedient which proved of great service on several occasions. A blockade-runner did not often pass through the fleet without receiving one or more shots, but these were always preceded by the flash of a calcium light, or by a blue light; and immediately followed by two rockets thrown in the direction of the blockade-runner. The signals were probably concerted each day for the ensuing night, as they appeared to be constantly changed; but the rockets were invariably sent up. I ordered a lot of rockets from New York.

Whenever all hands were called to run through the fleet, an officer was stationed alongside of me on the bridge with the rockets. One or two minutes after our immediate pursuer had sent up his rockets I would direct ours to be discharged at a right angle to our course. The whole fleet would be misled, for even if the vessel which had discovered us were not deceived, the rest of the fleet would be baffled.

While we were lying at anchor in the harbour of St. George's, during one of our trips, I was notified by the Governor of the island, that an officer of the Confederate Navy, then held as a prisoner on board one of H. B. M.'s ships of war at the naval anchorage, would be delivered up to me for transportation to the Confederacy, if I would assume the charge. This officer was charged with the murder of a messmate on board the Confederate States steamer *Sumter*, while lying at Gibraltar. The demand for his extradition, made by the Confederate Government, had been complied with by the British Government after much delay; and he was turned over to me for transportation to the Confederacy. Although the crime appeared to have been committed under circumstances of peculiar atrocity—it being alleged that the victim was asleep at the time he was shot—I so far respected the commission which the criminal bore, as to place him upon parole. Upon reporting his arrival at Wilmington to the Secretary of the Navy, the latter directed me to release him, upon the ground that it would be impossible to convict him by court-martial, all of the witnesses to the transaction being abroad. The man, Hester, was therefore released, and was never heard of again, I believe, during the war; but he has added to his evil reputation since its close, by plying the infamous trade (under the guise of United States Secret Service agent) of false informer and persecutor in several of the Southern States. The General Government failed to exercise its usual careful discrimination in making this appointment!

The base renegades are many degrees worse even than the unprincipled adventurers from the North who have so long preyed upon the South. The latter are only thieves and robbers; the former are, in addition, unnatural monsters, who hate their own people and are guilty of the crime of Judas, who betrayed his Lord for thirty pieces of silver.

CHAPTER 10

The *Lee* Escapes Capture

During the latter part of July, 1863, the *Lee* was lying in the harbour of St. George's, when the Confederate States steamer *Florida* arrived there in want of coal, of which there happened to be a very limited supply on hand. The most suitable coal was procured with difficulty throughout the war, all of the British coals, although excellent for raising steam, making more or less smoke, and objectionable on that account Exportation of the American anthracite, which would have been almost invaluable, was prohibited by the Government. This is, I believe, the only accessible, or at least available non-bituminous coal in the world; but the best substitute for it is the Welsh semi-bituminous coal, and this was chiefly used by the blockade-runners.

The *Florida* was in greater need of coal than ourselves, for the United States steamer *Wachusett* came into port a day or two after the former, and Maffitt, in command of the *Florida*, wished to get to sea first. When belligerent rights were accorded to the Confederate Government by foreign powers, the Confederate cruisers were admitted into their ports upon equal terms with the United States men of war, except that there was no interchange of *official* courtesies. In order to preserve strict neutrality toward the contending powers, a man of war under either flag was not permitted to follow out of a neutral port a ship under the enemy's colours within twenty-four hours of the sailing of the latter; and it was an equal violation of neutrality for a ship of war under either flag to cruise within a marine league of neutral territory.

When occasion required no one could be more resolute than Maffitt, as he had repeatedly shown in the management of the *Florida*; and especially when he ran the gauntlet in broad daylight through the whole Federal fleet blockading Mobile, and for which affair Preble, then commanding the fleet, was so harshly dealt with; but the chief object of the Confederate cruisers being to destroy the American commerce, an engagement with a United States ship of war was to be avoided, if possible.

The *Florida's* deck, when the crew were at their meals, was a curious scene; the plain fare of the sailors being served in costly china, captured from homeward bound "Indiamen," and the scamps had become fastidious in their taste about tea. I had the pleasure to carry into Wilmington ten or twelve chests of the finest hyson, which were distributed among the hospitals; and a lot of silver ingots made a narrow escape from confiscation. But the law officers in Bermuda, whom Maffitt consulted, assuring him that they would be adjudged legal prize of war in the British courts, they were shipped to England, instead of the Confederacy, and there returned to the claimants.

Although there was no exchange of civilities between the officers of the two ships, the sailors harmonized amiably and got drunk together ashore with mutual good will. A jack tar is probably the only representative left of the old "free lance," who served under any flag where he was sure of pay and booty. The blue jackets will fight under any colours, where there is a fair prospect of adventure and prize money.

After the *Florida* had been coaled, there was scarcely a sufficient supply left to carry the *Lee* into Wilmington under the most favourable circumstances; but it was necessary either to sail at once, or to wait two weeks for the next moon. Our chief engineer had noticed a large pile of coal on one of the wharves rented by the Confederate agent; but the heap had been so long exposed to the weather, and trampled upon for so many months, that it appeared to be a mere pile of dirt. "Necessity having no law," however, we shovelled off the surface; and were surprised to find that it was of very fair quality. It made an abundance of steam, indeed, but burned with great rapidity; and although we took on board an extra supply, we were able to retain barely enough English coal in the bunkers to use in running through the fleet on our next outward voyage. The consequence was the narrowest escape from capture ever made by the *Lee* while under my command.

We were ready to sail for Nassau on the 15th of August, 1863, and had on board, as usual, several passengers. Indeed we rarely made a trip either way without as many as could be accommodated, and many ladies among them. My observation of the conduct of the fair sex, under trying and novel circumstances, has convinced me that they face inevitable dangers more bravely and with more composure than men. I have frequently seen a frail, delicate woman standing erect and unflinching upon the deck, as the shells were whistling and bursting over us, while her lawful protector would be cowering "under the lee" of a cotton bale. I pay this humble tribute of admiration to the sex, but a cynical old bachelor, to whom I once made the observation, replied that in his opinion their insatiable curiosity prevailed even over their natural fears!

On our outward voyage we had among our passengers ex-Senator Gwin and his daughter, and Dr. and Mrs. P. We passed safely through the blockading fleet off the New Inlet Bar, receiving no damage from the few shots fired at us, and gained an offing from the coast of thirty miles by daylight. By this time our supply of English coal had been exhausted, and we were obliged to commence upon North Carolina coal of very inferior quality, and which smoked terribly. We commenced on this fuel a little after daylight.

Very soon afterwards the vigilant look-out at the masthead called out "Sail ho!" and in reply to the "where away" from the deck, sang out "Right astern, sir, and in chase." The morning was very clear. Going to the mast-head I could just discern the royal of the chaser; and before I left there, say in half an hour, her top-gallant sail showed above the horizon.

By this time the sun had risen in a cloudless sky. It was evident our pursuer would be alongside of us by mid-day at the rate we were then going. The first orders given were to throw overboard the deck-load of cotton and to make more steam. The latter proved to be more easily given than executed; the chief engineer reporting that it was impossible to make steam with the wretched stuff filled with slate and dirt. A moderate breeze from the north and east had been blowing ever since daylight and every stitch of canvas on board the square-rigged steamer in our wake was drawing. We were steering east by south, and it was clear that the chaser's advantages could only be neutralized either by bringing the *Lee* gradually head to wind or edging away to bring the wind aft.

The former course would be running toward the land, besides incurring the additional risk of being intercepted and captured by some of the inshore cruisers. I began to edge away therefore, and in two or three hours enjoyed the satisfaction of seeing our pursuer clew up and furl his sails. The breeze was still blowing as fresh as in the morning, but we were now running directly away from it, and the cruiser was going literally as fast as the wind, causing the sails to be rather a hindrance than a help. But she was still gaining on us.

A happy inspiration occurred to me when the case seemed hopeless. Sending for the chief engineer I said "Mr. S., let us try cotton, saturated with spirits of turpentine."

There were on board, as part of the deck load, thirty or forty barrels of "spirits." In a very few moments, a bale of cotton was ripped open, a barrel tapped, and buckets full of the saturated material passed down into the fire-room. The result exceeded our expectations. The chief engineer, an excitable little Frenchman from Charleston, very soon made his appearance on the bridge, his eyes sparkling with triumph, and reported a full head of steam. Curious to see the effect upon our speed, I directed him to wait a moment until the log was hove. I threw it myself, nine and a half knots.

"Let her go now sir!" I said.

Five minutes afterwards, I hove the log again, *thirteen and a quarter.* We now began to hold our own, and even to gain a little upon the chaser; but she was fearfully near, and I began to have visions of another residence at Fort Warren, as I saw the "big bone in the mouth" of our pertinacious friend, for she was near enough to us at one time for us to see distinctly the white curl of foam under her bows, called by that name among seamen. I wonder if they could have screwed another turn of speed out of her if they had known that the *Lee* had on board, in addition to her cargo of cotton, a large amount of gold shipped by the Confederate Government?

There continued to be a very slight change in our relative positions till about six o'clock in the afternoon, when the chief engineer again made his appearance, with a very ominous expression of countenance. He came to report that the burnt cotton had choked the flues, and that the steam was running down. "Only keep her going till dark, sir," I replied, "and we will give our pursuer the slip yet." A heavy bank was lying along the horizon to the south and east; and I saw a possible means of escape. At sunset the chaser was about four miles astern and gaining upon us. Calling two of my most reliable officers, I stationed one of them on each wheel-house, with glasses, directing them to let me know the instant they lost sight of the chaser in the growing darkness. At the same time, I ordered the chief engineer to make as black a smoke as possible, and to be in readiness to cut off the smoke, by closing the dampers instantly, when ordered. The twilight was soon succeeded by darkness. Both of the officers on the wheel house called out at the same moment, "We have lost sight of her," while a dense volume of smoke was streaming far in our wake.

"Close the dampers," I called out through the speaking

tube, and at the same moment ordered the helm "hard a star-board." Our course was altered eight points, at a right angle to the previous one.

I remained on deck an hour, and then retired to my state-room with a comfortable sense of security. We had fired so hard that the very planks on the bridge were almost scorching hot, and my feet were nearly blistered. I put them out of the window to cool, after taking off slippers and socks. While in this position, Miss Lucy G. came on the bridge in company with her father. Tapping my foot with her hand, she said, "Ah, captain, I see we are all safe, and I congratulate you!"

At one time during the chase, when capture seemed inevi-table, the kegs containing the gold had been brought on deck, and one of them opened by my orders, it being my intention to distribute its contents among the officers and crew. Miss Lucy, who preserved her presence of mind throughout the trying scenes of the day, called me aside, and suggested that she should fill a purse for me, and keep it about her person, until the prize crew had taken possession, and all danger of personal search was over, when she would make an opportu-nity to give it to me; and I have no doubt she would have ac-complished her intentions if occasion had required. The chaser proved afterwards to be the "Iroquois." Feeling confident that she would continue on the course toward Abaco, and perhaps have another and more successful chase, I changed the des-tination of the *Lee* to Bermuda, where we arrived safely two days afterward.

Upon the arrival of the *Lee* at Wilmington, after one more trip to Nassau, I was summoned by telegraph to Richmond. An attempt was to be made for the release of the prison-ers at Johnson's Island. This island, situated in the harbour of Sandusky, on Lake Erie, was supposed to be easily accessible from Canada, and the Canadian shore; but it was left to the judgment of the officer in command how the details were to be arranged, his sole explicit instructions being not to violate the neutrality of British territory.

How this was to be avoided has ever seemed impossible to me, but having been selected to command the expedition, I resolved to disregard all personal consequences, and to leave the responsibility to be borne by the Confederate Government. A party of twenty-six officers of the different grades was detailed for the service. The *Lee*, laden with a cargo of cotton, was to carry us to Halifax, N. S.; the cotton to be consigned to a firm there, who were to purchase, with a part of the proceeds, blankets, shoes, etc., for the army; the balance to be retained for the benefit of the prisoners, if released. My successor in command of the *Lee* took passage with us.

We sailed for Halifax on the night of October 10th, 1863. The season was so far advanced, that we could not afford to lose even a day; we therefore dropped down the Cape Fear River to Smithville as soon as the preparations were completed, and although the night was very clear, I determined to attempt the passage through the fleet soon after dark, so as to get as far north along the coast as possible before daylight. We crossed the western bar about nine o'clock at night, and instead of "hugging" the shore, which would have carried us too far to the southward and westward, the course was shaped so as to clear the Frying Pan Shoals.

We had been running at full speed for nearly an hour, when a shot came whizzing a few feet over our bulwarks, and struck the water just beyond us; it was followed immediately by another, which striking a little short "ricocheted" over us; and then a third, which crashing through the starboard bulwarks, burst in a cotton bale on the port side, and set fire to it; several men being wounded by splinters and fragments of the shells. The flames leaped high into the air, and there was a momentary confusion on board, but the order to throw the burning bale overboard was promptly executed, and for some time afterwards we could see it blazing far astern.

We never saw the cruiser which fired at us, as she was inshore, and although several more shots were fired, each succeeding one flew wider from the mark. We promptly sent up our two rockets abeam, and experienced no further trouble, easily avoiding a sloop of war cruising off the end of the Frying Pan Shoals. The fact is, a blockade-runner was almost as invisible at night as Harlequin in the pantomime. Nothing showed above the deck but the two short masts, and the smoke-stack; and the lead coloured hull could scarcely be seen at the distance of one hundred yards. Even in a clear day, they were not easily discovered.

Upon one occasion, when bound to Wilmington, we had crossed the Gulf Stream and struck soundings, when the look-out aloft reported a cruiser in sight ahead, and lying "*a-hull*" with her broadside exposed to us. It was evident, of course, that we were undiscovered so long as she lay in this position, and we continued to steam towards her, until we could plainly see her broadside guns. It was time for us to stop, but we preserved the same distance, undiscovered, for at least two hours. The engineer then reporting that the steam was running down, I directed him to fire up cautiously. The second shovel-full had scarcely been tossed into the furnace when a slight puff of smoke passed out of our smoke-stack, and at the same instant, the cruiser ahead wore round, and commenced a pursuit. There was clearly no want of vigilance on board of her.

But to return from this digression. By next morning we had got beyond dangerous waters. Some amusement was occasioned at the breakfast table by Johnny T., who had overheard the soliloquy of Colonel B. the night before. The Colonel, who was a member of the expedition, had seen service in the army of Northern Virginia. He was sitting upon the wheel house when the first shot was fired, and calmly remarked (to no one in particular,) "that is pretty firing," at the second "that is *very* pretty firing," and when the third shell burst upon the deck, he jumped upon his feet and exclaimed, with much emphasis, "if that isn't the prettiest firing I ever saw, I wish I may be d——d!"

CHAPTER 11
Captured

On our voyage to Halifax, we passed many vessels, and exciting no suspicion, for at that period many of the captured blockade-runners were afloat in the United States service. We showed American colours to those which passed near us and once, in thick weather off New York, we passed within hailing distance of a man of war bound South. We arrived at Halifax the 16th of October. The cargo of cotton was consigned to the firm of B. Wier & Co. with instructions to purchase shoes, etc., with a part of the proceeds, and to hold the balance to my credit.

There was then no agent of the Confederate Government in Halifax, but I had taken letters of introduction from a mercantile house in London to this firm to be used in case of touching there on the way back from Glasgow the year before. When I received my instructions from the Secretary of the Navy before leaving Richmond, I wished to ascertain to whom the cargo was to be consigned on our arrival at Halifax; and then learned from the Secretary of state, to whom I was referred, that there was no accredited agent of the government there.

In this dilemma I sought counsel of my good friend Mr. Seddon, Secretary of War, who advised me to act according to my own judgment. I therefore directed the bills of lading, invoices, etc., to be made out with B. Wier & Co. as consignees. In no case, I believe, did the Confederate Government appear as the shipper or consignor. Every cargo was supposed to be owned by private individuals; and the blockade-runners were regularly entered and cleared at the Confederate Custom House. Upon this occasion the *Lee*'s papers were closely scrutinized by the collector of the customs at Halifax, who did me the honour of personal attention; but he could find no flaw in them, and the vessel was regularly entered, with little more than the customary delay.

The *Lee* had made her last voyage under the Confederate flag. Sailing for Wilmington with a full cargo, she was captured off the coast of North Carolina. The land had been made the night before under quite favourable circumstances, but neither the captain, nor the pilot, being willing to assume the responsibility of taking charge of the vessel, the *Lee* was put to sea again, and by further culpable mismanagement, she fell an easy prey next morning to one of the United States cruisers. She had run the blockade twenty-one times while under my command, and had carried abroad between six thousand and seven thousand bales of cotton, worth at that time about two millions of dollars in gold, and had carried into the Confederacy equally valuable cargoes.

My staunch old helmsman, who had been released in New York by claiming British protection, and who started at once in search of me, met me in Halifax on our return from the Johnson's Island expedition. He actually shed tears as he narrated the train of circumstances which led to the capture. "She would have gone in by herself," he said, "if they had only let her alone;" for indeed it was evident to all on board the morning of her capture, that she had been close in to the shore within a few miles of the New Inlet Bar. She had not reached the bar, however, so that the pilot's course in refusing to take charge was justifiable; but the fatal error was committed by not making a good offing before daylight. At the time of her capture, she was not more than twenty miles from the land, and in the deep bay formed by the coast between Masonborough Inlet and the Cape Lookout Shoals.

The arrival of so large a party of Confederates in Halifax attracted attention, and it was essential to the successful execution of the project, that all suspicion should be allayed. The party, therefore, was divided into groups of three or four individuals, who were directed to report, in person, at Montreal, each one being strictly enjoined to secrecy and discretion; for although the precise object of the expedition was only known to three of its members, Lieutenants R. Minor, Ben. Loyall and myself, every one belonging to it was quite well aware that it was hostile to the United States Government. They were a set of gallant young fellows, with a single exception. Who he was and where he came from, none of us knew; but he had been ordered by the Secretary of the Navy to report to me for duty. We believed him to be a traitor and a spy; and succeeded in ridding ourselves of him the day after our arrival at Halifax, by advancing him a month's wages. No member of the expedition ever saw him again.

The most officiously zealous friend and partisan whom we all encountered in Halifax was Mr. "Sandy" Keith, who was facetiously called the Confederate Consul. By dint of a brazen assurance, a most obliging manner, and the lavish expenditure of money, *profusus sui alieni appetens*—he ingratiated himself with nearly every southerner who visited Halifax although he was a coarse, ill-bred vulgarian, of no social standing in the community. It is true that a worthy member of the same family had risen from obscurity to high honours, but Sandy was a black sheep of the flock.

He was employed at first by many of our people to purchase for them on commission, and afterwards by the Confederate Government. He profited by so good an opportunity for swindling, eventually forging invoices of articles, and drawing bills of exchange upon the Confederate Government, which were duly honoured. This villainy was perpetrated towards the end of the war, and at its close, Sandy Keith absconded with his ill-gotten gains, a considerable proportion consisting of money in his hands, belonging to private individuals.

Among his victims was Colonel S. of Baltimore, who determined to make an effort to recover his money. His first step was a visit to Halifax. His endeavours there to find Keith's whereabouts were for some time fruitless. But at last a clue was found. A girl, who had accompanied Keith in his flight, had written a letter to a relative in Halifax, and Colonel S. by some means obtained a sight of the envelope. The post-mark, plainly legible, indicated that the letter had been written at an obscure little village in Missouri. S. hastened back to Baltimore, and secured the cooperation of a detective, not for the purpose of arresting Keith, because he doubted whether he could recover possession of his property by the slippery and uncertain process of law, but for the sake of the detective's strong arm and presence of mind in the event of resistance. The reward to the detective being made contingent upon the recovery of the money, the pair left Baltimore, and in due time reached the village in the backwoods, where they learned that two persons, as man and wife, were boarding at the house of a widow, a mile or two distant.

They waited until night, and then, arming themselves with revolvers, started for the house of the widow. Knocking at the door, it was opened to them, and as they passed in, Keith's voice was heard, inquiring who had entered. Guided by the sound, they rushed to the room occupied by him. He had retired for the night. His loaded pistol was lying on a table near his bedside; but he had neglected to lock the door of his chamber, and S. and the detective had secured his arms and held him a prisoner before he was fairly awake. There was little parleying between them, the detective merely assuring him that if he did not come to terms speedily, his trunk would be broken open and all of its contents seized.

The whole affair was amicably settled in ten minutes, by a check upon the bank in which Keith had deposited some of his money, for the amount due to S., and the detective's reward. Keith demurred a little to the latter demand, but finally yielded to moral suasion; and next day S. presented the check, which was paid. Sandy Keith was supposed by those who had known him, to have been lost among the common herd of low swindlers and rogues, for none of them would have given him credit for enterprise or sagacity. He emerged, however, from obscurity, to perpetrate the most horrible and devilishly ingenious crime of the century; for it was he who under the name of Thomassen blew up the *City of Bremen* with his infernal machine.

Those who have read the account of that dreadful tragedy will remember that the explosion was precipitated by the fall of the box containing dynamite from a cart, or wheelbarrow, conveying it to the steamer. The hammer was set, by clockwork apparatus, to explode the dynamite after the departure of the steamer from England and when near mid-ocean, and Keith, confiding in the efficacy of the arrangement, was actually about to take passage in the steamer from Bremerhaven as far as England. Many persons believe that the *City of Boston* was destroyed some years ago by this incarnate fiend, and by the same means. That calamity carried mourning into many households in Keith's native city, for a large number of its most respectable citizens were on board. It will be remembered that she was supposed at the time to have foundered at sea in a gale of wind.

I had been furnished, before leaving Richmond, with letters to parties in Canada, who, it was believed, could give valuable aid to the expedition. To expedite matters, a trustworthy agent, a canny Scotchman, who had long served under my command, was dispatched to Montreal, via Portland, to notify these parties that we were on our way there. Our emissary, taking passage in a steamer bound to Portland, passed safely through United States territory, while the rest of us commenced our long and devious route through the British Provinces. Wherever we travelled, even through the remotest settlements, recruiting agents for the United States army were at work, scarcely affecting to disguise their occupation; and the walls of the obscurest country taverns bristled with advertisements like the following: "Wanted for a tannery in Maine one thousand tanners to whom a large bonus will be paid, etc." Many could not resist such allurements, but it was from this class and similar ones, no doubt, that the "bounty jumpers" sprang. It has been asserted, by those who were in a position to form a correct estimate, that the British Provinces, alone, contributed one hundred thousand men to the Federal army. It is scarcely an exaggeration to add, that the population of the civilized world was subsidized.

We were seven days in making the journey to Montreal, where my faithful agent met me by appointment, and carried me to the residence of Captain M., a zealous and self-sacrificing friend to the cause, and to whom I had been accredited. He looked steadily at me for a moment after our introduction, and then said "I have met you once before."

He recalled to my memory the fact, that while I commanded the battery at Acquia Creek in the early part of the war, he had brought a schooner loaded with arms, etc., up the Potomac, and succeeded in placing her under the protection of our batteries; having profited by a cold, dark, and inclement night, to evade the vigilance of the gunboats. Subsequently he and his family were compelled to leave Baltimore, and were now refugees in Canada.

Colonel K., also a refugee and an inmate of Captain M.'s house, and to whom, likewise, I carried letters, enlisted enthusiastically in the expedition, and devoted his whole time and energies to its success. We might, indeed, have obtained a large number of recruits from among refugees and escaped prisoners in Canada, but it was not considered prudent to increase the size of the party to any extent, our number being quite sufficient, under the plan as devised. But we picked up two or three escaped prisoners from Johnson's Island; among them an individual who was well known to Colonel Finney (a member of the expedition); having been in the Colonel's employment on the plains previous to the war. The Colonel was the right hand of Major Ficklin in organizing and putting into operation the "pony express," which used to traverse the continent from St. Louis to San Francisco, and our recruit, Thompson, was one of his trusted subordinates.

This man had led a very adventurous life. He informed us that after making his escape from Johnson's Island on the ice one dark winter night, he walked into Sandusky, and there laid in wait at the entrance of a dark alley for a victim with whom to exchange clothing. His patience being rewarded after a while, he laid violent hands upon his prize, and directed him to divest himself of his suit. The stranger replied, that he would not only supply him with clothing, but with money to make his way into Canada; adding that he had a son in the Confederate army. He gave Thompson the contents of his purse, and requesting him to wait till he could go home, soon returned with a full suit of clothes.

We had reliable information to the effect that the garrison at Johnson's Island was small, and that the United States sloop of war Michigan was anchored off the island as an additional guard. If the sloop of war could be carried by boarding, and her guns turned upon the garrison, the rest would be easy of accomplishment; and there appeared to be no obstacle to the seizure of as many vessels in Sandusky harbour, as might be required for purposes of transportation. They were to be towed over to the Canada shore, about twenty-five miles distant. There were several difficulties to be overcome; the chief one being how to notify the prisoners of the attempt about to be made. This was accomplished after several visits to Baltimore and Washington, by the brave and devoted Mrs. M. and her daughter; and finally the wife of General —— obtained permission from the authorities at Washington, to visit her husband, then a prisoner on Johnson's Island. Although the interview between them was brief, and in the presence of witnesses, she contrived to place in his hand a slip of paper, which informed him that our progress would appear in the *New York Herald's* "Personals" over certain initials, and so disguised as to be intelligible only to those who were initiated.

Next, it was important to know the exact condition of affairs in Sandusky, up to the time of our departure from Canada; and this was effected through the agency of a gallant gentleman, a retired British army officer, who went over to Sandusky upon the pretext of duck shooting, and who by a pre-arranged vocabulary, conveyed daily intelligence to us up to the time of our departure from Montreal. Everything progressed favourably, until we began to make final preparations for departure. Colonel K., who knew personally the manager of an English line of steamers upon the lakes, and confided in the integrity of the man, recommended him as most competent to give valuable information; and to him, under the seal of confidence, I applied. The only interview between us, (and in the presence of Colonel K.) was brief, and the object of the expedition was not divulged to him; nor was it intimated to him that any hostile act was contemplated; but he probably drew the inference. His replies to my questions were so unsatisfactory that I never saw him again, having recourse to other sources of information.

It was arranged that our party should take passage on board one of the American lake steamers at a little port on the Welland Canal. We were disguised as immigrants to the west; our arms being shipped as mining tools; and when clear of the canal, we were to rise upon the crew, and make our way to Sandusky. As the Michigan was anchored close to the main channel of the harbour, and we had provided ourselves with grapnels, it was believed that she could be carried by surprise. We had sent off our last "Personal" to the *New York Herald*, informing our friends at Johnson's Island "that the carriage would be at the door on or about the tenth;" our party had collected at the little port on the canal waiting for the steamer then nearly due, when a proclamation was issued by the Governor General, which fell among us like a thunderbolt.

It was announced in this proclamation, that it had come to the knowledge of the Government that a hostile expedition was about to embark from the Canada shores, and the infliction of divers pains and penalties was threatened against all concerned in the violation of the neutrality laws. What was even more fatal to our hopes, we learned that His Excellency had notified the United States Government of our contemplated expedition.

Our good friend sojourning at Sandusky abandoned his duck shooting in haste, (for the news sped across the frontier,) bringing intelligence that the garrison at Johnson's Island had been increased, and such other measures adopted as to render our success impossible. I called a council of the senior officers, who unanimously recommended that the attempt be abandoned; and so ended all our hopes. We learned, from what was believed by some to be a reliable source, that the informant against us was the manager, alluded to above, who betrayed us at the last moment.

There was a possibility of a successful issue to this enterprise, but not a probability. The American Consul at Halifax possessed intelligence and zeal; and he could easily have traced our course, by means of a detective, up to the very point of our departure on the Welland Canal. It is quite probable, indeed, that we were closely watched through the whole route, for immediately after the proclamation was issued, two or three detectives, no longer affecting disguise, dogged my footsteps for several days, with the intention I suspected of carrying me *vi et armis* across the frontier. But they were, in turn, subjected to as close an espionage by several members of the expedition, who were prepared for any emergency. "The engineer would have been hoisted with his own petard" probably, if they had attempted the arrest. That dare-devil Thompson, in fact, proposed one night that I should take a walk alone along the canal, and see what would come of it, but I declined the invitation.

One plan of releasing the Johnson's Island prisoners was to purchase a steamer in England, through the agency of Captain Bullock, load her with a cargo, and clear from the Custom House "for a market" on the lakes.—The chief obstacle to this plan would have been the passage, unsuspected, through the Welland Canal, but it was believed that, by proper discretion and management, this might have been accomplished, and the rest would have been easy; for all that was expected of any expedition was to carry the Michigan by surprise; the prisoners upon the island cooperating by attacking and overpowering the garrison.

As there was no farther necessity for keeping our movements secret, the whole party started together on the return to Halifax. We followed the route from Riviere du Loup overland by stage, or rather in sleighs, for the ground was already covered with snow, and the steamers had stopped running for the season, upon the beautiful picturesque St. John's River; and our way lay through a cheerless and sparsely populated country for nearly the whole distance. We were able too, without indiscretion, to accept the hospitalities of our friends in Halifax, during our brief stay there. But duty called us back to the Confederacy, and passage was engaged for the whole party by the first steamer (the *Alpha*) to sail for Bermuda.

CHAPTER 12

Back to the Confederacy

Arriving there, after a five or six day's voyage, we found many blockade-runners at anchor in St. George's harbour; and application was made to me to take command of one of them, called the *Whisper*, just out from England. She was a fair specimen of her class. Built expressly for speed and light draft, her frame was very slight, but she was a capital sea boat, and made several successful trips. There was a striking contrast, however, between her and the solidly built, magnificent *Lee*. After all arrangements had been completed for the transportation to the Confederacy of our party, I assumed command of the little *Whisper*, with six or eight of the party as passengers. I remember my astonishment at learning the rates for freight at this period. The *Whisper* was loaded and ready for sea, and I was dining with Mr. Campbell, the agent of the company, when a person asked to see him upon pressing business. The purpose of the visitor was, to ship by the *Whisper* a small lot of medicines. As the vessel was already heavily laden, Mr. Campbell referred him to me, and I consented to take the box in the cabin. The freight upon it was £500 sterling![9]

Six blockade-runners, including the *Whisper*, sailed for Wilmington within twenty-four hours of each other. The voyage across was stormy, and the sky so overcast as to compel us to run by dead-reckoning, until we had crossed the Gulf Stream, early on the third day. We had been steaming against a strong gale the whole time. These cold north-westers brought disaster upon many blockade-runners; for blowing over the tepid water of the Gulf Stream, clouds of vapour would rise like steam, and be condensed by the cold wind into a fog so dense as to obscure every object.

At such times, the skill and perseverance of the navigator would be taxed to the utmost. A glimpse of the sun, moon, or north star, caught through the sextant wet with spray, and brought down to a most uncertain horizon, would furnish the only means of guidance, where an error of a few miles in the calculation would probably prove fatal. Upon reaching soundings on the western edge of the "stream," about eleven o'clock in the forenoon, we succeeded in catching a glimpse of the sun, and thus ascertaining our position.

The sea was still running very high, but the weather had moderated considerably, and we found ourselves not more than forty miles south-east of the western bar. The *Whisper* had fared badly, while running in the teeth of the gale; all of our boats, except one, had been swept from the davits, and the wheel houses had been stove in. As there was no further necessity to strain the hull and engines, the little craft was brought near the wind under low steam, and close-reefed mainsail; riding the long rolling seas like a sea-gull. To windward the sky soon became clear, but we took care not to get far away from the dense fog to leeward of us. We did not see a cruiser, while we lay for many hours anxiously waiting for night.

As the sun set, the order was given to go at full speed, and before midnight we had passed safely through the blockading fleet, and had come to anchor off Smithville. Out of the six steamers which sailed from St. George's, the *Whisper* alone succeeded in getting in. Most of them were run ashore, and their cargoes partially saved; but some fell, intact, into the hands of the vigilant cruisers.

After a few weeks' service on board the ill-fated ironclad, built in Wilmington, I was summoned by telegram to Richmond. The Confederate authorities were then projecting an attempt to release the Point Lookout prisoners. There appeared to be no insuperable obstacle in the way; and it was believed that the prisoners, if released, and furnished with arms, would be able to join the forces under the command of General Early, then in the vicinity.

Two steamers of light draft were to be loaded with arms, etc., and were to carry, in addition to their crews, an infantry force under the command of General Custis Lee. In the event of success, the steamers were to be burned.

On my way to Richmond, my life was saved by the presence of mind of my faithful servant, Essex, who accompanied me on a visit to his home in Virginia. General Wilson had just made a very destructive raid along the line of the Richmond and Danville Railroad, striking the road at Burkeville, and effectually damaging it as far as Meherrin Bridge, a distance of thirty miles or more, where his progress was stopped. He did not return within General Grant's lines without heavy loss; and when I arrived at Ream's Station, on the Petersburg and Weldon road, I found there a strong force of Confederate cavalry, under General Chambliss, waiting to intercept the retreat.

As I was bearer of dispatches from General Whiting to General Lee, a hand car, with two men to work it, was detailed for me, and with my servant on board we started to run the gauntlet between the lines. The distance to be accomplished was about seven miles, and we had passed over more than half of it, when one of our videttes suddenly made his appearance, and we halted to inquire about the state of affairs ahead. His report was satisfactory, and we started again, but had only gone a short distance when we saw a squad of cavalry, which we supposed to be part of General Wilson's force, charging rapidly after us.

The highway lay close alongside the railroad, and our pursuers were enveloped in a cloud of dust. The car was stopped, or rather the men who were working the crank incontinently took to their heels, and we followed their example. There was a fence a few rods from the road, which I succeeded in reaching, and over which I jumped, just before our pursuers overtook us. As they forced their horses over it, I discovered my friend, the vidette among them, who cried out as he saw me "*That* is General Wilson, kill him?" and I have not the least doubt his advice would have been followed, but for Essex, who cried out from a snug corner, where he was ensconced, "For God's sake, don't shoot! He is one of your best friends!"

They lowered their pistols, and I had an opportunity to explain matters. My gold watch and chain had probably excited the cupidity of my friend above mentioned. I admit that I felt uncharitable towards him, and when I hinted my suspicions of his motives to the officer in command of the squad, he did not deny the probability of a cause for them, but seemed to consider me unreasonable in expecting to find *all* the virtues in a "high private," who was receiving scanty fare, and $8 a month in Confederate money! The party escorted us within the lines.

After all the details of the expedition had been arranged in Richmond, the naval portion of it was ordered to Wilmington under my command. On our journey, we followed the route previously pursued by the raiders from Burkeville to Meherrin Bridge. Nearly every foot of the way was marked by evidences of the havoc of war; and the air was tainted with the stench from the dead horses and mules, whose throats had been cut when they could travel no farther.

There were sufficient reasons why I took no subsequent part in the expedition, the naval portion of it being placed under the command of Captain J. T. Wood, of the Confederate States Navy and also one of the President's aids. It failed, however, owing to the fact that secretly as all the preparations had been made, information of it was speedily conveyed to the authorities at Washington, and prompt measures taken to prevent its success. The steamers had dropped down the Cape Fear River, and were on the very point of putting to sea when countermanding orders were telegraphed from Richmond;

for the Confederate Government, through their secret sources of information, had been promptly notified of the fact that the plot had been betrayed to the United States authorities. How the Federal Government obtained its intelligence will, perhaps, forever remain a mystery to the public; but there was a very general belief in the Confederacy, that an individual near the President was a paid traitor to the cause.

These futile projects for the release of prisoners, serve to show the desperate straits to which the Confederacy was reduced, for want of soldiers.

It was deemed expedient, at this period, to re-establish the light on Smith's Island, which had been discontinued ever since the commencement of hostilities; and to erect a structure for a light on the Mound. At the beginning of the war, nearly all of the lights along the Southern coast had been discontinued; the apparatus being removed to places of safety.

Under special instructions, I was charged with the duties of relighting the approaches to the Cape Fear River, and of detailing pilots, and signal officers to the blockade-runners. To provide the means of light, every blockade-runner was required to bring in a barrel of sperm oil. In addition to these aids to navigation, the signal stations were extended farther along the coast, and compulsory service was required of the pilots. Owing to the constantly increasing vigilance of the blockading fleet, and the accession to the navy of fast cruisers, many prizes had been captured of late. Their pilots were, of course, held as prisoners of war; and the demand for those available for service, increasing in proportion to their diminished number, there was much competition between the rival companies, to the great detriment of the public service.[10] It was considered necessary, therefore, to establish an office of "Orders and Detail" at Wilmington, whence should proceed all orders and assignments in relation to pilots and signal officers. In a short time, the benefit of these arrangements was very perceptible. The blockade-runners were never delayed for want of a pilot, and the casualties were much diminished.

The staid old town of Wilmington was turned "topsy turvy" during the war. Here resorted the speculators from all parts of the South, to attend the weekly auctions of imported cargoes; and the town was infested with rogues and desperadoes, who made a livelihood by robbery and murder. It was unsafe to venture into the suburbs at night, and even in daylight, there were frequent conflicts in the public streets, between the crews of the steamers in port and the soldiers stationed in the town, in which knives and pistols would be freely used; and not infrequently a dead body would rise to the surface of the water in one of the docks with marks of violence upon it. The civil authorities were powerless to prevent crime. *Inter arma silent leges!*

The agents and employees of the different blockade-running companies, lived in magnificent style, paying a king's ransom (in Confederate money) for their household expenses, and nearly monopolizing the supplies in the country market. Towards the end of the war, indeed, fresh provisions were almost beyond the reach of every one. Our family servant, newly arrived from the country in Virginia, would sometimes return from market with an empty basket, having flatly refused to pay what he called "such nonsense prices" for a bit of fresh beef, or a handful of vegetables. A quarter of lamb, at the time of which I now write, sold for $100, a pound of tea for $500. Confederate money which in September, 1861, was nearly equal to specie in value, had declined in September 1862 to 225; in the same month, in 1863, to 400, and before September, 1864, to 2000!

Many of the permanent residents of the town had gone into the country, letting their houses at enormous prices; those who were compelled to remain kept themselves much secluded; the ladies rarely being seen upon the more public streets. Many of the fast young officers belonging to the army would get an occasional leave to come to Wilmington; and would live at free quarters on board the blockade-runners, or at one of the numerous bachelor halls ashore.

The convalescent soldiers from the Virginia hospitals were

sent by the route through Wilmington to their homes in the South. The ladies of the town were organized by Mrs. De R. into a society for the purpose of ministering to the wants of these poor sufferers; the trains which carried them stopping an hour or two at the depot, that their wounds might be dressed, and food and medicine supplied to them. These self-sacrificing, heroic women patiently and faithfully performed the offices of hospital nurses.

O! there are angels in this world unheeded,
Who, when their earthly labour is laid down,
Will soar aloft, with pinions unimpeded,
And wear their starry glory like a crown!

Liberal contributions were made by companies and individuals to this society, and the long tables at the depot were spread with delicacies for the sick, to be found nowhere else in the Confederacy. The remains of the meals were carried by the ladies to a camp of mere boys—home guards outside of the town. Some of these children were scarcely able to carry a musket, and were altogether unable to endure the exposure and fatigues of field service; and they suffered fearfully from measles, and typhoid fever. General Grant used a strong figure of speech, when he asserted, that "the cradle and the grave were robbed, to recruit the Confederate armies." The fact of a fearful drain upon the population was scarcely exaggerated, but with this difference in the metaphor, that those who were verging upon both the cradle and the grave, shared the hardships and dangers of war, with equal self-devotion to the cause. It is true that a class of heartless speculators infested the country, who profited by the scarcity of all sorts of supplies, but it makes the self-sacrifice of the mass of the Southern people more conspicuous, and no state made more liberal voluntary contributions to the armies, or furnished better soldiers, than North Carolina.

When General A. P. Hill asked for the promotion of some of his officers in June, 1863, the President laid down the rule of selection for the guidance of the Secretary of War, *viz*: "the state which had the greatest number of regiments should be entitled to the choice of positions; to be taken from the candidates of its citizens, according to qualifications," etc. It appeared that North Carolina stood first on the list, Virginia second, Georgia third, etc.

On the opposite side of the river from Wilmington, on a low marshy flat, were erected the steam cotton presses, and there the blockade-runners took in their cargoes. Sentries were posted on the wharves, day and night, to prevent deserters from getting on board, and stowing themselves away; and the additional precaution of fumigating the outward bound steamers at Smithville, was adopted; but in spite of this vigilance, many persons succeeded in getting a free passage abroad.

These deserters, or "stowaways," were in most instances sheltered by one or more of the crew; in which event they kept their places of concealment until the steamer had arrived at her port of destination, when they would profit by the first opportunity to leave the vessel undiscovered. A small bribe would tempt the average blockade-running sailor to connive at this means of escape. The "impecunious" deserter fared more hardly; and would, usually, be forced by hunger and thirst to emerge from his hiding place, while the steamer was on the outward voyage. A cruel device, employed by one of the captains, effectually put a stop, I believe, certainly a check to the escape of this class of "stowaways." He turned three or four of them adrift in the Gulf Stream, in an open boat, with a pair of oars, and a few days' allowance of bread and water.

The ironclad, to which I had been attached for a short time, made her first and last essay while I was on special duty at Wilmington. Having crossed New Inlet Bar early one morning, she steamed at her best speed towards the blockading-fleet, which kept beyond the range of her guns with much ease. After "raising the blockade" for an hour or two, she steamed back across the bar, grounded upon the "rip," broke her back, and doubtless remains there to this day, buried fathoms deep in the quicksands.

The prospects of the South were growing more and more gloomy with each succeeding day; and the last hopes of the country now rested upon that gallant army of Northern Virginia, which, under its great captain, still confronted General Grant's forces around Petersburg. It is easy now by the light of subsequent events to censure Mr. Davis for the removal of General Johnston from the command of the army in Georgia; but who does not remember how, previous to that unfortunate measure, the whole Southern press, almost without an exception, were urging it? It may be that the President was not indisposed to gratify his inclination, and at the same time appease the public. I do not presume to express an opinion on this point; being no partisan of either, but a sincere admirer of both these distinguished individuals, and crediting both with strict veracity and unselfish honesty of purpose. But the fact remains that the press teemed with articles denouncing General Johnston's retrograde movements.

A spurious telegram, concocted by some facetious editor, to the effect that General Johnston had ordered means of transportation for his army to Nassau, was circulated through all the newspapers for the public amusement. But the old army officers were shocked at the intelligence of his removal from command. When the fact was officially announced, all of them, whom I had an opportunity of hearing speak upon the subject, expressed the gravest fears of the consequences; General Whiting, especially, declaring his conviction that it was a fatal measure; and it is certain that General Johnston's army was enthusiastically devoted to him; officers and men, with few exceptions, reposing unbounded confidence in him.

Concurrent testimony has since conclusively proven how grave a mistake was committed. General Hooker, who served in that campaign under General Sherman, writes:

This retreat was so masterly, that I regard it as a useful lesson for study for all persons who may hereafter elect for their calling the profession of arms. . . . The news that General Johnston had been removed from the command of the army opposed to us, was received by our officers with universal rejoicing. . . . One of the prominent historians of the Confederacy ascribes the misfortunes of the 'Lost Cause' to the relief of General Johnston. I do not think this, but it certainly contributed materially to hasten its collapse.

Indeed the Confederate Government seems subsequently to have admitted its mistake, and the injustice inflicted upon General Johnston, by reinstating him in the command of the "army of the South," and with orders "to concentrate all available forces, and drive back Sherman." This, however, was not till February, 1865, when the "available forces" amounted to about 16,000 men, and General Sherman's army of 70,000, had reached the state of North Carolina unopposed.

When General Johnston turned over the command to General Hood, the army consisted of 36,900 infantry 3,750 artillery, and 9,970 cavalry, a total of 50,620 well equipped troops.

In returning from its disastrous expedition against Nashville, the army of Tennessee had halted in northeastern Mississippi. A large proportion of these troops were then furloughed by General Hood, and went to their homes. When General Sherman's army invaded South Carolina, General Beauregard ordered those remaining on duty to repair to that state. . . . The remaining troops of that army were coming through Georgia in little parties. . . . at least two-thirds of the arms of these troops had been lost in Tennessee.[11]

In General Johnston's Narrative, he says:

The troops themselves, who had been seventy-four days in the immediate presence of the enemy, labouring and fighting daily; enduring trial and encountering dangers with equal cheerfulness; more confident and high-spirited even than when the Federal army presented itself before them at Dalton; and though I say it, full of devotion to him who had commanded them, and belief of ultimate success in the campaign, were then inferior to none who ever served the Confederacy, or fought on the Continent. . . . I believed then, as firmly as I do now, that the system pursued was the only one at my command, that promised success, and that, if adhered to, would have given us success.

Many among those most competent to judge entertained the same conviction. His removal from the command was, indeed, a mortal blow to the cause.

NOTES

9. Mr. Campbell had given me a bill of exchange for just this amount to take command of the steamer during the inward trip. As the *Whisper* belonged to a private company, I accepted the bonus without scruple. What became of it, and the value of Confederate currency at that time may be seen by the following:

Invoice of 123 bales cotton purchased and stored at Columbus, Georgia, for account of Captain John Wilkinson.
Feb. 27, 1864. By W. W. Garrard.

2 Bales weighing	1,085 lbs
4 Bales weighing	2,219 lbs
5 Bales weighing	3,241 lbs
5 Bales weighing	2,655 lbs
107 Bales weighing	52,833 lbs
62,033 lbs at 72-5/8	$45,051.46
Charges	
state tax on investment	$225.26
Commission for purchasing	$2252.57
C. S. war tax	$337.89
	$2815.72
E. & O. E.	$47,867.18

Signed, *Power, Low & Co*
Wilmington, March 2, 1864
Captain J. Wilkinson
In acc. with Power, Low & Co
March 2, 1864
To Invoice 123 bales cotton at Columbus, Georgia $47,867.18

Cr. Feb. 17. By proceeds W. L. Campbell's	$46,666.66
Exchange on London £500 at 2100	
Balance due us	$1,200.52

Wilmington, March 2, 1864. Signed, *Power, Low & Co*

"The cotton was destroyed at the very close of the war by a party of raiders commanded, I believe, by General Wilson. If he were the same individual for whom I was once mistaken (as will be seen in the sequel) he served me two very ill turns."

10. One or two agents of the blockade-running companies were opposed to any project for increasing the facilities of entrance to or exit from Wilmington. The profits were of course proportionate to the risks, and these heartless worshipers of Mammon, having secured the services of the best captains and pilots, would have rejoiced to see every blockade-runner, but their own, captured. They protested vehemently, but unavailingly, against interference with their pilots.

11. General Johnston's Narrative. It appears from the same distinguished authority that of all that gallant array not more than 5,000 were ever reassembled; and a large portion of these continued without arms to the end of the war.

CHAPTER 13

Fog

In the latter part of September, 1864, I was ordered to the command of the *Chickamauga*, a double screw steamer converted into a so-called man of war. She was one of those vessels before alluded to in this narrative, as partly owned by the Confederate Government, and was taken possession of by the government authorities with scant regard for the rights of the other owners, who had no alternative but to accept inadequate compensation for their share of the vessel.

Her battery consisted of a twelve-pounder rifled gun forward, a sixty-four pounder amidships, and a thirty-two pounder rifle aft, all on pivots. She was more substantially built than most of the blockade-runners, and was very swift, but altogether unfit for a cruiser, as she could only keep the sea while her supply of coal lasted. She was schooner rigged, with very short masts, and her sails were chiefly serviceable to steady her in a sea-way. Under all sail and *off* the wind, without steam, she could not make more than three knots with a stiff breeze; *by* the wind under the same circumstances, she had not even steerage way.

Captain J. T. Wood, of the Confederate Navy, had just returned from a "raid" along the Northern coast, and the incompetent Secretary of the Navy conceived, no doubt, that he had hit upon a happy idea when it occurred to his muddled brain, to send these vessels out to harass the coasting trade and fisheries of the North.[12] As a mere question of policy, it would have been far better to have kept them employed carrying out cotton and bringing in the supplies of which the army was so sorely in need. The attack upon Fort Fisher was probably precipitated by these expeditions, which could in no wise affect the real issues of the war. But Mr. Mallory was from first to last an incubus upon the country. I do not impugn his patriotism, nor his private character, but his official imbecility, which wrought much damage to the cause, is a legitimate object for censure.

At this period Atlanta had been captured, and a large portion of Georgia was practically severed from the Confederacy. It was becoming more and more difficult to provision the troops. The Subsistence Department of the Confederate Government has been often censured for its alleged mismanagement. I have personal knowledge of an instance where it resented the interference of a subordinate. Major Magruder, General Whiting's chief Commissary, had effected what he believed to be a mutually beneficial arrangement with the farmers of western North Carolina. He was to furnish salt and transportation, (the former a very rare and costly commodity at that time, and the latter difficult to be obtained); and in return, they were to supply his department with the cured bacon. The arrangement, when reported to the Department at Richmond, was cancelled, and the Major, a very zealous and competent officer, was ordered elsewhere.

Surely there must have been grave mismanagement somewhere; for, several months after the period of which I now write, and when the army of Northern Virginia was almost reduced to starvation in February, 1865, there were stored "in the principal railroad depots between Charlotte, Danville and Weldon inclusive, rations for 60,000 men for more than four months," and these provisions were for the exclusive use of the army in Virginia. The fact was ascertained by taking account of those stores, which was done by order of General Johnston:

. . . . and the very zealous and efficient officer, Major Charles Carrington, who was at the head of the service of collecting provisions in North Carolina for the army, was increasing the quantity rapidly. . . . The officers of the commissariat in North Carolina, upon whom the army in Virginia depended for subsistence, were instructed by the Commissary General just then, to permit none of the provisions they collected to be used by the troops serving in it.[13]

We sailed in the *Chickamauga* on the night of October 29th, with a motley crew, and passed through the blockading fleet without receiving any damage from numerous shots. We had a fine view of several of our pursuers for a few moments, as they burned their signal blue light; and had not crossed the bar two hours before the commanding officer of the fleet received information of the fact. Our rockets had diverted the pursuit to the misfortune of the blockade-runner *Lady Stirling*, which was captured; and from some of her crew, as we subsequently learned, the fact of our departure was ascertained.

If we could have foreseen such an event, we might have tried the range of our after pivot gun with very good effect upon the blockader following in our wake; but although our crew was at quarters, and we were prepared to fight our way to sea, we wished to avoid an encounter by which nothing was to be gained; our chief object being to injure the enemy's commerce. Nearly all of the officers of the *Chickamauga* had resigned from the United States Navy, and I have no doubt they contrasted (as I could not help doing) next morning, our spar deck encumbered with coal bags, and begrimed with dirt, and the ragged tatterdemalions leaning over the bulwarks, or stretched along the decks in the agonies of sea-sickness, with the cleanliness, order and discipline, to which we had been accustomed under the "Stars and Stripes."

The condition below decks was even worse; the crew sleeping upon the coal which was stowed in the hold; and the officers upon the softest plank they could find in the contracted cabin. In addition to a complement of officers for a frigate, the Secretary of the Navy had ordered *six* pilots to the vessel. As three of them held their "branches" for the approaches to Norfolk, Mr. Mallory must have expected to hear that we had passed under the guns of Fortress Monroe, laid Norfolk under contribution, and captured the Gosport Navy-yard.

The scene upon our decks, when the sun rose the morning after our passage through the fleet, was demoralizing; and I am sure some of us felt as if we were indeed "pirates," although we were bound to deny the "soft impeachment," when brought against us by the Northern press. The exertions of the executive officer, Dozier, seconded by his zealous subordinates, brought some degree of order out of this "chaotic" mass after a while.

Our first prize was the *Mark L. Potter*, from Bangor for Key West, with a cargo of lumber. As there was no alternative but to destroy her, the officers and crew were transferred to the *Chickamauga*, and she was set on fire. This capture was made on Sunday the 30th. The next morning at 7.30 a.m., when about one hundred and fifty miles off the Capes of Delaware, we sighted a square-rigged vessel, which changed her course in the effort to escape, as soon as she discovered that we were steering for her. At 9.30 we overhauled her and brought her to. It proved to be the barque *Emma L. Hall*, loaded with a cargo of sugar and molasses. She was set on fire at 11.15 a.m. Hasty work was made of this prize, as a full rigged ship hove in sight while we were transferring the crew, and such stores as we needed, from the *Emma L. Hall*.

The stranger bore north by west when discovered, and was standing almost directly toward us, with studding-sails and royals set to the favourable breeze, a cloud of snowy canvas from her graceful hull to the trucks of her tapering royalmasts. She approached within five or six miles, when her studding-sails were suddenly hauled down, and she was brought close to the wind in an effort to escape from us. We soon overhauled her, and at 1.15 were near enough to throw a shot across her bow, and to show the Confederate flag at our peak. The summons was replied to by their hoisting the Stars and Stripes, and heaving to. Our prize was the clipper ship *Shooting Star*, bound from New York to Panama, with a cargo of coal for the U. S. Pacific squadron.

While we were making preparations for burning her, another square rigged vessel hove in sight, steering toward us. It proved to be the barque *Albion Lincoln*, bound for Havana, partly in ballast; and as her cargo consisted only of a small lot of potatoes and onions, I determined to bond her, and to put the prisoners, now numbering sixty (the wife of the captain of the *Shooting Star* among them) on board of her. In truth, I was relieved from an awkward dilemma by the opportune capture of the *Albion Lincoln*; for there was absolutely no place for a female on board the *Chickamauga*. I do not doubt, however, that the redoubtable Mrs. Drinkwater would have accommodated herself to the circumstances by turning me out of my own cabin. Heavens! what a tongue she wielded! The young officers of the *Chickamauga* relieved each other in boat duty to and fro; and she routed every one of them ignominiously.

After the *Albion Lincoln* had been bonded for $18,000, we were kept very busy for several hours paroling prisoners, etc., and in the meanwhile a gale of wind was brewing, and the sea growing very rough. By six o'clock in the afternoon, the *Lincoln* was under way with the paroled prisoners; her master having been put under oath to shape the vessel's course for Fortress Monroe; and we applied the torch to the *Shooting Star*. The burning ship was visible for many miles after we left her; and it was a strange, wild spectacle, that flaming beacon in the rough sea. The master of the *Albion Lincoln* shaped his course straight for New York. I hope his conscience has since reproached him for violating his oath, though given to a "rebel."

The gale increased during the night. Next day our course was shaped for Montauk Point; the scene of the previous day's operations having been in about latitude 40° and longitude 71°, or about fifty miles southeast of Sandy Hook. Montauk Point was sighted from aloft about mid-day, and the engines were slowed down, so as not to approach too near the land before night. We spoke several vessels during the day, all of them under the British flag. Toward night we steamed towards the land, with the expectation of finding smoother water, for the wind continued to blow from the southwest.

At 5.45 p.m., we overhauled two schooners close in to the shore; one of them was the *Goodspeed*, from Boston to Philadelphia, in ballast; and the other, the *Otter Rock*, from Bangor for Washington with a load of potatoes. Both were scuttled. Our boats did not get alongside the *Chickamauga* again till eight o'clock. The wind had been gradually veering round to the northeast, and the night was growing so dark and stormy, that I was reluctantly compelled to abandon the purpose previously entertained of entering Long Island Sound. The crew of the *Goodspeed* profited by the darkness to escape in their boat to the land, a few miles distant.

We made an offing of thirty or forty miles during the night, and next morning captured the bark *Speedwell*, in ballast from Boston to Philadelphia. The captain's sister and his child were on board his vessel, and represented to be sick. I could not reconcile it to my sense of humanity to subject the weaker sex to the probable dangers and certain hardships of confinement on board the *Chickamauga*. The *Speedwell* was therefore bonded for $18,000, and the captain—a very decent fellow by the way—sent on his voyage rejoicing; but the "recording angels" of the Northern press never placed this act to my credit.

The northeast gale, which had been brewing for some days, commenced in earnest toward the evening. After buffeting against it for two days, the necessity for making a port became apparent, our supply of coal beginning to get low. The course was, therefore, shaped for Bermuda, and we anchored off the bar at St. George's on Monday morning, November 7th.

The Governor of the island gave us a vast deal of trouble and annoyance, from this time until we finally left port. Lending apparently a willing ear to the representation of the American Consul, he would not permit us to enter the harbour until after a correspondence, in which I stated the fact that our engines needed repairs; but we lay outside twenty-four hours before even this permission was granted. He next forbade me to coal the ship. After a protest from me he relented so far, only, as to authorize a supply of coal, sufficient to carry the *Chickamauga* to the nearest Confederate port, although he had been officially informed that the vessel was regularly commissioned, and was then on a cruise.

Although I was never favoured with a sight of the correspondence, which must have been carried on between the American Consul and His Excellency on the subject, I am satisfied that the former presented a favourable case; but the Governor had no right to inquire into the antecedents of the *Chickamauga*, or to question the title by which she was held by the Confederate Government. She was, to all intents and purposes, as *bona fide* a man-of-war as the *Florida*, which had entered that same port, and been supplied with coal, and other necessaries, without question or molestation. But the fortunes of the Confederacy were now waning; and his Excellency wished perhaps—and may have received instructions—to keep on good terms with the winning side, and in disregard of the obligations of justice to the weaker party.[14]

The result of his partial, and unfriendly course, was to bring the cruise of the *Chickamauga* to a speedy end; for it was impossible for her to keep the sea without a supply of fuel—steam, which is merely an auxiliary in a properly constituted man of war, being the *Chickamauga*'s sole motive power. Many of our crew, too, were enticed to desert; but the efficiency of the vessel was rather increased than diminished by our getting rid of the vagabonds. They were for the most part "waifs and strays," of Wilmington, and "skulkers" from the army, who had been drafted from the Receiving ship. They profited by liberty on shore to secrete themselves, and many of them perished with the yellow fever, then prevailing in Bermuda.

We sailed from St. George's for Wilmington November 15th, showing our colours to several vessels on the way, all of which carried a foreign flag. American colours had for a long time become a rare sight upon the ocean, except when flying from the peak of a man-of-war. All of the vessels captured by the *Chickamauga* were either coasters, or traders to West India ports, and were scarcely off soundings on the American coast.[15]

The *Alabama* and *Florida* had demonstrated what a vast amount of injury might be inflicted upon an enemy's commerce by a few swift cruisers; and there is no doubt that this number might have been increased to any reasonable extent, by proper management. No sensible individual, I presume, really attaches any importance to the ravings of a portion of the Northern press, during the war, against the "rebel pirates," and their depredations upon commerce.

To destroy merchant vessels was not a pleasure, but it was a duty, and a matter of necessity, seeing that the Confederate ports were so closely blockaded as to render it absolutely impossible to send the prizes in for adjudication, and that all of the foreign powers prohibited the sending of captured vessels into their ports. The officers and crews attached to these "piratical vessels" would very gladly have carried or sent their prizes into a Confederate port; for in that case they would have been equally fortunate with their confreres of the United States Navy, whose pockets were filled to repletion with the proceeds of captured property belonging to Confederates, on land and sea.

We approached the coast in very thick weather on the night of the 18th. We could dimly discern the breakers ahead, and close aboard; but it was impossible to distinguish any landmark in so dense a fog. A boat was lowered therefore, and one of the bar pilots sent to examine nearer, but he returned on board in the course of an hour, with the report that he had pulled close in to the surf, but could recognize no object on the shore, although he had rowed some distance parallel to it, and as closely as he could venture.

"Did you see no wrecks on the beach?" I inquired.

"Yes, sir," he replied, "I saw three."

"And how were they lying?" I asked.

He stated that two of them were "broadside on" to the beach, and close together; and the third "bows on" to the beach, about a cable's length to the north of them. I was satisfied about our exact position at once, for while I was on the special service before alluded to, I had made a visit to Masonborough Inlet, on duty connected with the signal stations, and had noticed three wrecks in the positions described. The *Chickamauga* was put under low steam, with one watch at quarters, and we waited for daylight to cross the bar.

As the fog lifted, shortly after sunrise, two of the blockading fleet were discovered on our port quarter, steaming towards us, as we were running down the coast towards Fort Fisher. When within long range they opened fire, which was returned by us. They were soon joined by a third blockader, and as we drew nearer to the bar, Fort Fisher took part in the engagement, and the blockaders hauled off. Shortly afterwards we crossed the bar, and anchored inside of the "Rip."

Notes

12. It is very far from my intention, by these remarks, to condemn the depredations of the Confederate cruisers upon the Federal commerce, or the policy which dictated the fitting of them out. But there appears to me to be a wide difference between the destruction of ships and cargoes belonging to capitalists, who contributed by their means and influence to the support of the Federal Government, and the burning of fishing craft manned by poor men, who relied upon the "catch" of the trip for the means of feeding and clothing their families. But I will not expatiate upon the "sentiment" involved in the subject, for fear of incurring the reproach cast by Sir Peter Teazle upon that very humane and sentimental character, Joseph Surface, whose actions differed so widely from his words.

13. From General Johnston's Narrative.

14. But there was a striking contrast during the war, between the conduct of the British officials, acting in their official capacity, towards the Confederate officers, and that of individuals belonging to both branches of Her Majesty's service; the latter, almost without an exception, expressed their cordial sympathy with the south, and extended many acts of courtesy and good feeling towards us, but the former scrupulously abstained from every semblance of recognition or of sympathy.

15. The Shooting Star was an exception, she being chartered by the government.

CHAPTER 14

The End Draws Near

Another, and a longer cruise, was then contemplated, and there was some prospect of prevailing with the Secretary of the Navy to fit out the ship for a cruiser, by giving her proper spars, providing the means of disconnecting the screws, and furnishing quarters for officers and men. But disasters to our arms were then following fast upon each other. General Sherman, after marching unopposed from Atlanta to the sea, and capturing Savannah, was preparing to continue his progress. Wilmington was threatened by a powerful sea and land force. The half starved and ill clad army of Northern Virginia was in the trenches around Petersburg, and the now contracting area of country available for supplies, had been so thoroughly drained, that it became a vital question how to provision the troops.

I was summoned again, and for the last time during the war, to Richmond. It was in the early part of December. There now remained to the Confederacy only the single line of rail communication from Wilmington, via Greensborough, and Danville, to Richmond. The progress of demoralization was too evident at every step of my journey, and nowhere were the poverty, and the straits to which the country was reduced, more palpably visible, than in the rickety, windowless, filthy cars, travelling six or eight miles an hour, over the worn out rails and decaying road-bed. We were eighteen hours in making the distance (about one hundred and twenty miles) from Danville to Richmond.

As we passed in the rear of General Lee's lines, and I saw the scare-crow cattle there being slaughtered for the troops, the game seemed to be at last growing desperate. We were detained for perhaps an hour at the station where the cattle were being slaughtered. Several soldiers who were on the train, left us there; and as soon as they alighted from the cars, they seized portions of the offal, kindled a fire, charred the scraps upon the points of their ramrods, and devoured the unclean food with the avidity of famished tigers.

It was arranged in Richmond, that I should take command of the *Tallahassee*, and proceed with all dispatch to Bermuda for a cargo of provisions; my late experience with the Governor of the island rendering it quite probable that he would prevent the *Chickamauga* from even discharging her cargo as a merchant vessel. That steamer (the *Tallahassee*) of so many aliases, had just returned from a short cruise under Captain Ward of the Confederate States Navy. She was now christened again, and bore, thenceforward, the appropriate name of the *Chameleon*. Her battery was dismounted, the officers and crew detached, and she was ostensibly sold to the navy agent at Wilmington. A register, and bill of sale, were prepared in legal form, the crew shipped according to the laws relating to the merchant service, and regular invoices and bills of lading made out of her cargo of cotton. The vessel, indeed, was so thoroughly whitewashed, that she subsequently passed a searching examination in Bermuda; but my recent experience there had convinced me of the necessity of adopting every precaution, and I was left to my own discretion with regard to all the details; the instructions under which I was acting requiring me only to bring in a cargo of provisions with all dispatch.

The *Chameleon* was in nearly all respects like the *Chickamauga*, only a few feet longer, and drawing a few inches more water.

On the afternoon of December 24th, the United States fleet opened fire upon Fort Fisher, the heavy cannonading continuing during the two following days. The booming of the heavy guns could be distinctly heard in Wilmington.

There was a complete panic there; the non-combatants moving away, and fright and confusion prevailing everywhere. The co-operating land forces, under General Butler, had almost completely invested the fort, and the communication between it and Wilmington was at one time interrupted, so that it was impossible to ascertain the condition of affairs below. In the midst of the turmoil, we cast off from the wharf, about two o'clock in the afternoon of December 26th, and anchored off Smithville after dark, the tide not serving for crossing the bar that night.

Next morning the *Agnes Fry*, an inward bound blockade-runner, was discovered aground on the western bar. Towards evening two or three of the blockading fleet stationed off that bar steamed in, and opened fire upon her. The bombardment of the fort was still in progress. A little after dark, just as we were weighing our anchor, General Whiting, who was then in Fort Fisher, telegraphed to us that the United States land forces were embarking, the attack upon the fort having been abandoned. We were under way in a few moments, closely followed by the *Hansa*, Captain Murray, and parting from her just as we crossed the bar. I had known the captain for many months, under his assumed name, and it was quite generally known that he held a commission in the British Navy.

While I was living in Nova Scotia, some years afterwards, the card of Captain A. commanding H. B. M. ship *J——n* was brought to me, and I was surprised to find in the owner of it, my old friend Murray. Several British naval officers of rank and high character, were engaged in the same exciting and lucrative occupation of blockade-running; among them the gallant Captain Burgoyne, who commanded afterwards the unfortunate ship *Captain* of H. B. M.'s Navy, and who perished together with nearly the whole crew when she foundered at sea.

We crossed the bar under such favourable circumstances,

that we were not discovered; nor did we see any of the fleet until we had cleared the Frying Pan Shoals, when we easily avoided several vessels which had participated, no doubt, in the attack upon Fort Fisher, and were now about to take their stations off the western bar.

We made a rapid, though a very rough voyage to Bermuda, a stormy northwest gale following us nearly the whole distance. The Prussian Major von Borcke, who had served on General Jeb Stewart's staff, and who afterwards published, in *Blackwood's*, his experience of the war, was a passenger. The Major was no sailor, and his sufferings from sea sickness were much aggravated by a gunshot wound in his throat. As the engines of the *Chameleon* would "race" in the heavy sea following us, and her whole frame would vibrate, he declared in military phraseology ("our army swore terribly in Flanders!") that he would rather encounter the dangers of a "stricken field" than voluntarily endure an hour of such torture.

We arrived at St. George's on the 30th of December; and our troubles immediately commenced. It was the 5th of January before permission was received to land our cargo of cotton; His Excellency, the Governor having called upon the law officers of the crown for aid in the dire dilemma. When the vessel's papers were at last pronounced correct, we discharged our cargo, and then arose the perplexing question of loading. I haven't the least doubt that the American Consul was sadly bothering His Excellency all this time; but permission was finally granted to us to take in provisions but no munitions of war. As we did not want "hardware," as munitions of war were then invoiced, we proceeded to load. But a great deal of time had been lost, and we did not take our departure for Wilmington till January the 19th; having on board as passengers General Preston and staff, returning from Europe.

Our voyage across was very rough, and the night of our approach to New Inlet Bar was dark and rainy. Between one and two o'clock in the morning, as we were feeling our way with the lead, a light was discovered nearly ahead and a short distance from us. As we drew closer in and "sheered" the Chameleon, so as to bring the light abeam, I directed our signal officer to make the regular signal. No reply was made to it, although many lights now began to appear looming up through the drizzling rain.

These were undoubtedly camp fires of the United States troops outside of Fort Fisher; but it never occurred to me as possible, that a second attack could have been made, and successfully in the brief period of time which had elapsed since our departure from Wilmington. Believing that I had made some error in my day's observations, the *Chameleon* was put to sea again, as the most prudent course in the emergency. The night was too far spent to allow of any delay. Orders were therefore given to go at full speed, and by daylight we had made an offing of forty or fifty miles from the coast.

Clear and pleasant weather enabled me to establish our position accurately—it was my invariable custom, at sea, during the war, to take my own observations—and early in the night we made the Mound Light ahead, for which I had shaped our course. The range lights were showing, and we crossed the bar without interference, but without a suspicion of anything wrong, as it would occasionally happen, under particularly favourable circumstances, that we would cross the bar without even seeing a blockader. We were under the guns of Fort Fisher in fact, and close to the fleet of United States vessels, which had crossed the bar after the fall of the fort, when I directed my signal officer to communicate with the shore station.

His signal was promptly answered, but turning to me, he said, "No Confederate signal officer there, sir; he cannot reply to me."

The order to wear round was instantly obeyed; not a moment too soon, for the bow of the Chameleon was scarcely pointed for the bar before two of the light cruisers were plainly visible in pursuit, steaming with all speed to intercept us. Nothing saved us from capture but the twin screws, which enabled our steamer to turn as upon a pivot in the narrow channel between the bar and the "rip." We reached the bar before our pursuers, and were soon lost to their sight in the darkness outside. Our supply of coal being limited, the course was shaped for Nassau as the nearer port, where we arrived without accident. A day or two after our arrival the news came of the fall of Fort Fisher.

Several narrow escapes, besides our own, were made. Maffitt, in command of the *Owl* crossed the Western Bar a night or two after the fall of Fort Fisher, and while our troops were evacuating Fort Caswell and other military stations along the river. Crossing the bar, and suspecting no danger, he continued on his way up to Smithville, where he anchored. He was boarded a few moments afterwards by a boat from our military post there. The officer in command of the boat informed him of the capture of Fort Fisher, and that our troops were then evacuating Fort Caswell; adding that several vessels of the Federal fleet had crossed the New Inlet Bar, and were at anchor in the river almost within hail of him. Maffitt was about to give the order to slip the chain, "not standing upon the order of his going," when his pilot begged for permission to go ashore, if only for ten minutes. He represented the situation of his wife, whom he had left ill and without means of support, in such moving terms, that Maffitt granted permission, upon condition that he would return speedily. The pilot was faithful to his promise, returning in fifteen or twenty minutes. During his absence, steam was raised, and the chain unshackled. As the pilot's foot touched the deck of the *Owl* again, the boat was hooked on and run up to the davits, the chain slipped, and the *Owl* on her way to sea again.

Another blockade-runner is said to have been not so fortunate. She had run the gauntlet safely, and come to anchor off Smithville. The tarpaulins had been removed from the hatches, the lamps lighted, and a cold supper spread upon the table, at which the passengers were seated, two or three officers of the British army among them. A toast to the captain had been proposed, and they had just tossed off a bumper in champagne to his health and continued successes, and he was about to reply to the compliment, when the officer of the deck reported that a boat was coming alongside. The captain received the officer at the gangway. The mail bag, according to the usual routine, was given to the latter for transportation to the shore; and the customary inquiries made after the name of the vessel, cargo, number of passengers, etc. The astounded captain was then informed that his vessel was a prize to the United States ship—then at anchor near him!

Charleston was now the only harbour on the Atlantic coast at all accessible, and that must evidently soon fall; but a cargo might be landed there before that inevitable catastrophe, and fully appreciating the exigency, I determined to make the effort. Even after the occupation of Wilmington by the United States troops, there would remain an interior line of communication between Charleston and Virginia. The facts of history prove that the importance of carrying in a cargo of provisions was not exaggerated, for the army of northern Virginia was shortly afterwards literally starving; and during their retreat from the position around Petersburg the country adjacent to their line of march was swarming with soldiers who had left the ranks in search of food.

But it was the part of prudence to ascertain, positively, before sailing, that Charleston was still in our possession. This intelligence was brought by the *Chicora* which arrived at Nassau on the 30th of January; and on February 1st, the *Owl*, *Carolina*, *Dream*, *Chicora* and *Chameleon* sailed within a few hours of each other for Charleston.

The condition of affairs throughout the Confederacy was far more desperate than we, who were abroad, had any idea of. Despondency and demoralization had advanced with gigantic strides within the past two or three eventful months. Admiral Semmes, in his *Memoirs of Service Afloat, etc*, gives the following account of an interview with General Lee:

As soon as I could command a leisure moment, I paid General Lee a visit at his head-quarters near Petersburg, and spent a night with him. I had served with him in the Mexican War. We discussed together the critical state of the country and of his army—we were now near the end of January, 1865, and I thought the grand old chieftain and Christian gentleman seemed to foreshadow in his conversation, more by manner than by words, the approaching downfall of the cause for which we were both struggling. I had come to him, I told him, to speak of what I had seen of the people, and of the army, in my transit across the country, and to say to him that unless prompt measures could be devised to put an end to the desertions that were going on among our troops, our cause must inevitably be lost. He did not seem to be at all surprised at the revelations I made. He knew all about the condition of the country, civil and military, but seemed to feel himself powerless to prevent the downward tendency of things, and he was right. It was no longer in the power of any one man to save the country. The body politic was already dead. The people themselves had given up the contest, and this being the case, no army could do more than retard the catastrophe for a few months. Besides, his army itself was melting away. That very night, as I learned at the breakfast table, one hundred and sixty men deserted in a body. It was useless to attempt to shoot deserters when demoralization had gone to this extent.

A few weeks subsequent to the date referred to in the above extract, General Johnston was ordered to "drive back Sherman." He states in his *Narrative* in reference to accepting the command:

This was done with a full consciousness on my part, however, that we could have no other object in continuing the war than to obtain fair terms of peace; for the Southern cause must have appeared hopeless then to all intelligent and dispassionate Southern men.

We passed Abaco light soon after dark, and shaped our course direct for Charleston. At early dawn the next morning, while I was lying awake in my room on the bridge, I heard the officer of the deck give the quick sharp order to the helmsman "hard a-port!" The steering wheel in all of the blockade-runners was upon the bridge and immediately forward of the captain's state-room, and the officer of the deck kept his watch upon the bridge.

As I never undressed at night, while at sea in command during the war, I was out upon the deck in a moment; and then I saw distant two or three miles and directly in our former course, a large side-wheel steamer. From her size and rig, I guessed her to be the *Vanderbilt*; and I was afraid that the Chameleon had at last found more than her match, for the *Vanderbilt* enjoyed the reputation of great speed. We wore round before we were discovered, but as the strange steamer's bow was pointed in our direction a few moments afterwards, it was plain that we would have to make good use of our heels, and that the race would be a trying one.

The *Chameleon* was in fine condition for the ordeal, and the usual precaution of cleaning fires, and raising the steam had been taken before daylight. My staunch old quartermaster, McLean, who had been with me in nearly all the chances and changes of blockade-running, always took his place at the wheel on trying occasions. He had nerves of steel, and would have steered the vessel without flinching against a line of battle ship, if so ordered. Upon one occasion, after we had crossed the Western Bar, and were steaming at full speed along the coast, we suddenly discovered a long low blockader on our starboard bow, and at the same instant, distinctly heard the order from the stranger's deck, to "pass along the shell!"

I called out to my old helmsman, "Port and run her down!" and if the strange vessel had not moved out of our way with alacrity, she would have been assuredly cut in two. We grazed her stern by a hair's breadth as we shot by her at the rate of thirteen knots. Before they had recovered from the confusion on board of her, we had passed into the darkness beyond, and the shell which they sent after us flew wide of its mark.

McLean was now placed at the wheel. It was a close race for hours, neither apparently gaining or losing a foot; but Providence again befriended us. As the day advanced, the breeze, which was very light from the northward at daylight, continued to freshen from that quarter. We soon set all of our canvas, and so did the chaser, but as the latter was square rigged, and we carried fore and aft sails, our sheets were hauled flat aft, and the *Chameleon* kept close to the wind by the steady old helmsman. I do not doubt that we would have been over-hauled but for this favourable contingency. Head to wind our pursuer would certainly have overtaken us, and off the wind her chances would have been almost equally good. But she began to drop gradually to leeward as the wind continued steady, and by two o'clock in the afternoon, she was five or six miles distant on our lee quarter. Although we had not in-creased the distance between us much, if any, since the com-mencement of the chase, we had weathered upon the chaser until her sails had become useless about twelve o'clock when she furled them.

As the snowy cloud of canvas was rolled up like magic, and the tall tapering spars were seen in its place, I supposed the cruiser was about to retire from the contest; but she still fol-lowed with the tenacity of a bloodhound. But apparently to no purpose till about two o'clock, when the chief engineer, Mr. Schroeder, appeared on the bridge with the report that the journals were heated, and it was absolutely necessary to stop to ease the bearings!

This was a predicament, indeed; but when I looked down into the hold, and saw the clouds of vapour rising from the overheated journals, as a stream of water was being pumped upon them, I saw that Schroeder was right in the assertion, that unless the bearings were instantly eased, the machinery would give way. I had implicit confidence in Schroeder, and it had been justly earned, for he had served long under my command, and had always displayed, under trying circumstances, great coolness, presence of mind, and ability. He made every preparation for the work before him, taking off his own coat, and when everything was in readiness, the order to stop the engines was given.

In a few moments, we lay like a log upon the water, and the chaser was rapidly lessening the distance between as, and the suspense became almost intolerable. Our fate was hanging by a thread; but in ten minutes the journals had been cooled off, the bearings eased, and the *Chameleon* again sprang ahead with renewed speed. The steamer in chase had approached nearly within cannon shot—probably within long range—but in the course of the next hour, we had gained so rapidly in the race that the pursuit was abandoned as hopeless; and as the stranger wore around, to resume her station under easy steam, we followed in her wake till dark, when we evaded her without difficulty, and continued on our course toward Charleston.

But another precious day had been lost, and subsequent unfavourable weather still further retarding our progress, we did not reach the coast near Charleston Bar till the fifth night after our departure from Nassau. The blockading fleet had been reinforced by all the light cruisers from the approaches to the Cape Fear River; and as we drew in to the land, we were so frequently compelled to alter the course of the Chameleon, in order to evade the blockaders, that we did not reach the bar till long after midnight, and after the tide had commenced to fall. I was tempted to force the pilot to make the attempt, but finally yielded to his assurances that access was impossible under the circumstances. As this was the last night during that moon, when the bar could be crossed during the dark hours, the course of the *Chameleon* was again, and for the last time, shaped for Nassau. As we turned away from the land, our hearts sank within us, while the conviction forced itself upon us, that the cause for which so much blood had been shed, so many miseries bravely endured, and so many sacrifices cheerfully made, was about to perish at last!

CHAPTER 15

Richmond Captured

Arriving at Nassau on the 8th, we found many blockade-runners in port, waiting for news from Charleston; and on the 10th, the *Owl* returned, after an unsuccessful attempt to enter Charleston, during which she received a shot through her bows; and intelligence came also of the capture of the *Stag* and *Charlotte*. On the 23rd, the *Chicora*, which had succeeded in getting into Charleston, arrived with the fatal news of its evacuation, and the progress of General Sherman through Georgia and South Carolina. This sad intelligence put an end to all our hopes, and we were now cut off from all communication with the Confederate Government authorities.

In this dilemma, Maffitt and I consulted with Mr. Heyliger, the Confederate agent at Nassau; and it was decided that the *Chameleon* should be taken over to England. Whatever might be the course of events, our duty appeared to be to turn our vessels over, either to the agent of the Navy Department in Liverpool, or to the firm of Messrs. Fraser, Trenholm & Co. there. We learned afterwards, indeed, that Captain Pembroke Jones, of the Confederate Navy, was at that time on his way to us via Galveston or Mexico, with orders from the Navy Department. All of us were directed to take in cargoes of provisions to a specified point on the Rappahannock River, under the protection of Confederate artillery to be stationed there in readiness. The steamers were to be burned after landing their cargoes, but Jones could not reach us in time.

The bottom of the Chameleon being quite foul, divers were employed to scrub it preparatory to her long sea voyage. These people are wonderfully expert, remaining under the surface nearly two minutes; and the water in the harbour of Nassau is so clear that they can be distinctly seen even at the keel of a vessel.

Our cargo of provisions was landed, and an extra supply of coal taken on board. The vessel being under Confederate colours and liable to capture wherever found, except in neutral waters, it behoved us to be prepared at all times to show our heels to a stranger Some of our crew who wished their discharge, for the purpose of rejoining their families at the South, were paid off; the rest of them shipped for the voyage to Liverpool via Bermuda. We still lingered for later intelligence which was brought by the mail steamer *Corsica* from New York.

Charleston was evacuated on the 17th of February, and Fort Anderson, the last of the defences at Wilmington, fell on the 19th. General Johnston had assumed command of the broken remnant of the army of the Tennessee in North Carolina, and subsequently offered some resistance to the hitherto unimpeded march of General Sherman; but the latter was now about to effect a junction with General Schofield, who commanded a large force which had landed at Wilmington. It was too evident that the end was near.

The speculators in Nassau saw that "the bottom had fallen out," and all of them were in the depths of despair. Some of them, it is true, had risen from the desperately hazardous game with large gains, but the majority had staked their all and lost it; and even the fortunate ones had contracted a thirst for rash ventures, which eventually led to the pecuniary and social ruin of some of them. Even the negro stevedores and labourers bewailed our misfortunes, for they knew that the glory of Nassau had departed forever.

My old friend Captain Dick Watkins probably more un-selfishly regretted the disasters to our arms than the speculators or even the refugees in Nassau, who had succeeded in evading service in the army by skulking abroad. A recruiting officer might have "conscripted" nearly a brigade of the swaggering blusterers. Captain Dick and I parted with mutual regret; and I sincerely hope, if Providence has been pleased to remove the old fellow's helpmeet to a better sphere, that he has found consolation in a virtuous union with one of those "mighty pretty yaller gals" he so much admired; and that Napoleon Bonaparte may rise to the highest dignities in that parti-coloured community of spongers and "wrackers."

We sailed from Nassau on the 22d of March and arrived at St. George's, Bermuda on the 26th. The harbour was deserted, and the town, in its listless inactivity, presented a striking contrast with its late stir and bustle. After coaling, we took our departure for Liverpool on the 26th of March, and arrived there on the 9th of April. It was Palm Sunday, and the chimes were ringing sweetly from the church bells, as we came to anchor.

The contrast between this happy, peaceful, prosperous country and our own desolated, war-distracted land, struck a chill to our saddened hearts. The last act in the bloody drama was about to close on that very day at Appomattox Court House, and before that sun had set, the Confederate Government had become a thing of the past.

We, who were abroad, were not unprepared for the final catastrophe; for we had learned on our arrival at Liverpool of General Early's defeat in the valley of the Shenandoah, and the accession to General Grant's already overwhelmingly large forces of General Sheridan's cavalry; and of the junction of General Sherman with General Schofield. To oppose these mighty armies, there were 33,000 half starved, ragged heroes in the trenches around Petersburg, and about 25,000 under General Johnston in North Carolina.

This may not be a proper place to allude to the fearful penalties inflicted upon a people who fought and suffered for what they deemed a holy cause. But it should be proclaimed, in the interest of truth and justice, that the South since the close of the war, has been preyed upon by un-principled adventurers and renegades who are determined to rule or ruin. But a brighter day will come. Calumny and injustice cannot triumph forever. That distinguished officer Colonel C. C. Chesney of the British army in a volume of military biography lately published by him, in allusion to General Lee, writes thus:

> But though America has learned to pardon, she has yet to attain the full reconciliation for which the dead hero would have sacrificed a hundred lives. Time can only bring this to a land, which in her agony, bled at every pore. Time, the healer of all wounds will bring it yet. The day will come, when the evil passions of the great civil strife will sleep in oblivion, and North and South do justice to each other's motives, and forget each other's wrongs. Then history will speak with clear voice of the deeds done on either side, and the citizens of the whole Union do justice to the memories of the dead.

Surely all honest men and true patriots will rejoice to see that day.

The firm of Fraser, Trenholm & Co. was represented in Liverpool by a Mr. Prioleau who was by no means anxious for the consignment of the *Chameleon* in ballast; with a cargo on board the case would have been different. He evidently considered her a very big and un-saleable elephant, and repudiated the part of showman. The vessel was therefore turned over to Captain Bullock, who acted with his usual tact and discretion in the subsequent transactions connected with her. There was a sharp struggle between rival claimants for the possession of the ship, but the Gordian knot was cut by the British Government which placed the "broad arrow" upon her. The public funds were also transferred to Captain Bullock and his receipt taken for them.

Here I beg leave to affirm that I neither appropriated nor desired to appropriate any of the spoils of the perishing ship of state.[16] But as memory recalls the many opportunities placed in my way of making a fortune during the war, without detriment to the cause, and consistent with every obligation due to the Confederate Government, there are times when I cannot decide whether I acted the part of a fool, or that of a patriot. We are told that when Lord Clive was arraigned before the British Parliament for profiting by his high position in India to enrich himself, he exclaimed at the close of his defence against the charge, "By G——d, Mr. Chairman, at this moment I stand astonished at my own moderation!" His idea of "moderation" was £300,000. A "dead broke" Confederate would have considered himself fortunate to possess 300,000 cents!

Some of the crew of the *Chameleon*, who had served for years in the Confederate Navy, brought a claim against me for pay due them while in the public service, and it was with some difficulty that their counsel, a pettifogging lawyer, could be induced to consent to arbitration; but the matter was finally settled through Bullock's agency, although it appeared probable at one time that I would be obliged to take a hasty departure from England.

The end was close at hand. News of the capture of Richmond arrived on the 15th, and a few days afterwards, intelligence of the surrender of General Lee's army.

The *Chameleon* was soon afterwards given up to the United States Government which claimed the assets, but repudiated the liabilities of the Confederate Government. Her officers and crew were turned adrift with "the wide world before them where to choose."

Notes

16. The proofs, which I hold in my possession, of this affirmation can have no interest for the general reader. Shortly after the close of the war, I learned through a friend in Washington that I was charged with appropriating many thousands of dollars belonging to the late Confederate Government. Although I was then living in Halifax, Nova Scotia, and beyond the

jurisdiction of the United States Government, I forwarded to the Hon. Secretary of the United States Navy, copies of the receipts taken by me from Captain Bullock, in Liverpool, for all Confederate property in my possession. I may be permitted indeed, to claim eminent disinterestedness, for I might have accumulated a fortune; and at the end, my faithful and efficient paymaster, E. Courtenay Jenkins, a gentleman of the purest integrity, made the transfer by my direction; both of us washing our hands of the "filthy lucre," and retaining a clear conscience.

ALSO FROM LEONAUR
AVAILABLE IN SOFTCOVER OR HARDCOVER WITH DUST JACKET

SEPOYS, SIEGE & STORM *by Charles John Griffiths*—The Experiences of a young officer of H.M.'s 61st Regiment at Ferozepore, Delhi ridge and at the fall of Delhi during the Indian mutiny 1857.

CAMPAIGNING IN ZULULAND *by W. E. Montague*—Experiences on campaign during the Zulu war of 1879 with the 94th Regiment.

THE STORY OF THE GUIDES *by G. J. Younghusband*—The Exploits of the Soldiers of the famous Indian Army Regiment from the northwest frontier 1847 - 1900..

ZULU: 1879 *by D.C.F. Moodie & the Leonaur Editors*—The Anglo-Zulu War of 1879 from contemporary sources: First Hand Accounts, Interviews, Dispatches, Official Documents & Newspaper Reports.

THE RECOLLECTIONS OF SKINNER OF SKINNER'S HORSE *by James Skinner*—James Skinner and his 'Yellow Boys' Irregular cavalry in the wars of India between the British, Mahratta, Rajput, Mogul, Sikh & Pindarree Forces.

TOMMY ATKINS' WAR STORIES 14 FIRST HAND ACCOUNTS—Fourteen first hand accounts from the ranks of the British Army during Queen Victoria's Empire Original & True Battle Stories Recollections of the Indian Mutiny With the 49th in the Crimea With the Guards in Egypt The Charge of the Six Hundred With Wolseley in Ashanti Alma, Inkermann and Magdala With the Gunners at Tel-el-Kebir Russian Guns and Indian Rebels Rough Work in the Crimea In the Maori Rising Facing the Zulus From Sebastopol to Lucknow Sent to Save Gordon On the March to Chitral Tommy by Rudyard Kipling

CHASSEUR OF 1914 *by Marcel Dupont*—Experiences of the twilight of the French Light Cavalry by a young officer during the early battles of the great war in Europe.

TROOP HORSE & TRENCH *by R. A. Lloyd*—The experiences of a British Lifeguardsman of the household cavalry fighting on the western front during the First World War 1914-18.

THE EAST AFRICAN MOUNTED RIFLES *by C. J. Wilson*—Experiences of the campaign in the East African bush during the First World War.

THE FIGHTING CAMELIERS *by Frank Reid*—The exploits of the Imperial Camel Corps in the desert and Palestine campaigns of the First World War.

www.ingramcontent.com/pod-product-compliance
Lightning Source LLC
Chambersburg PA
CBHW030755150426
42813CB00068B/3110/J